**A Gift of
The Institute for the Study of
Human Knowledge**

SUFISM AND THE ISLAMIC TRADITION:

THE LAMAHAT AND SATA'AT OF SHAH WALIULLAH

Sufism and The Islamic Tradition:
The Lamahat and Sata'at of Shah Waliullah

Translated by G. N. Jalbani
and Edited by D. B. Fry

The Octagon Press
London

THE LAMAHAT AND SATA'AT

"Lamahat" (Flashes or Glimpses of Philosophy) is the most famous work of Shah Waliullah on philosophy. It begins with an exhaustive treatment of the word "Being" (*Wujud*), and the author has shown that by it is meant the Reality and not the concept or an idea. Some other subjects, like Al-Shakhs Al-Akbar (*Ash-Shakhs al-Akbar*, the Great Body), Hazirat Al-Quds (*Huwiyyat*, The Holy Fold), the various classes of angels and the different forms of the emanations (*Tajalliyat*) are also thoroughly discussed.

He has explained fully the reality of Invention (*Ibda'a*), Creation (*Khalq*), Administration (*Tadbir*) and the Emanation (*Tadalli*) by means of which the Divinity works in the Universe. In the knowledge of the different capabilities of human individuals, their expected perfection and their end, Shah Sahib excels almost all his predecessors. He has indeed given a detailed account and a clear exposition of these subjects.[1]

The original copy of this treatise is most probably lying in the Jamiat Al-Milliyyah Library, in Delhi. There was, however, a hand-written copy of it in the Mazhar Al-Ulum Madrasah in Karachi. This was not compared with the original one when it was published by the Shah Waliullah Academy. Thus some mistakes remained. A year after its publication, an Urdu translation of it made by Pir Muhammad Hasan was published in the April and October 1964 issues of *Iqbal*, a Journal of Bazm-i-Iqbal, Lahore. The Urdu translation when consulted was not found free from mistakes, but in spite of that, credit goes to the translator for his having made a beginning.

Thereafter a modest attempt was made by the present

---

[1] Al-Juzu'-Al-Latif.

translator to render "Lamahat" in English. Care has been taken to remove ambiguity wherever it was noticed, but with all that, it cannot claim to be completely free from it.

The philosophical views of Shah Waliullah are scattered in his works. If any continuity of them is maintained, it is found in his two small treatises "Lamahat" and "Sata'at", to both of which reference has been made in glowing terms by his grandson Shah Ismail Shahid in the introduction to his celebrated work "Abaqat". On the strength of these two treatises in particular, he has given preference to him over Ibn Al-'Arabi and Imam Rabbani. It is hoped this translation may be found interesting and useful.

"Sata'at" is one of the famous works of Shah Waliullah on mystical philosophy. Though it is a small treatise, it throws sufficient light on the subject. It mostly deals with the life after death and the system of Divine manifestations working in the universe. What chiefly characterises this treatise is the frequent quotations from the Qur'an in support of the argument the author has advanced.

It is, however, essential to note that Shah Waliullah believed in the doctrine of the Unity of Being (*Wahdat al-Wujud*), and this doctrine is the central point round which his whole system of philosophy works. The reason why he is always attempting to evolve co-ordination among various religions as far as it is possible is that this doctrine has a place in one form or the other in almost all religions. An example of such an attempt at co-ordination can be seen in Sat' 45.

He explains the significance of "Being" in the beginning, but an exhaustive account of it is given in "Lamahat", his other most celebrated work on the same subject. These two small books in particular cover a considerable part of his philosophy. Shah Isma'il Shaheed, the grandson of Shah Waliullah, in the introduction to his "Abaqat" has spoken highly of these two works, and on the strength of them has claimed his superiority over Ash-Shaikh Al-Akbar Ibn Al-'Arabi. The last Sat' on the interpretation of the "Verse of light" may be taken as the text and all the remaining ones as its commentary.

I am greatly obliged to Dr. Nabi Bakhsh Qazi, Head of the Department of Persian in the University of Sind, for his having reviewed the translation. It is hoped that this English version, when read with the original text, may be found informative and useful.

G. N. JALBANI
Professor and Head of the Department
of Arabic, University of Sind,
Hyderabad, Pakistan.

CONTENTS

LAMAHAT

LAMAHAT

All praise is due to God, the Lord of the worlds. Blessings and benedictions be on the Chief of the Prophets, on his family and his Companions.

Lamha 1

Every effect is originated (*Hadith*), as its cause precedes it. Every originated is transformable, because it is preceded by its originator, its transformer.

Every compound of two things is preceded by its parts; and every thing the actuality and the individuality of which are actualised, is preceded by its actuality, the essence (*Huwiyyat*) of which is that species, and by its individuality, the essence of which is that individual.

It is, therefore, necessary that the First and the Origin of all should not be an effect, nor an origination, nor an actualised one from any essence and any individual.

Lamha 2

It should not be imagined that the First of the first is one individual of the Being (*Wujud*), and that the Being has included it as the whole includes its individual parts. Nay, the First of the first has encompassed this universal and all-embracing conception of the Being, from above, from below and from all its sides. It is so because this conception of the Being precedes it when those realities which are the sources of many different consequences (*Athar*) are considered in general. In this way, however, the Being is distinguished from the Not-Being. But the reality of the Being is not distinguished from other realities. This consideration has, therefore, created a

form in the brain named Being, while as a matter of fact
all the realities return to the First and sink in it. Therefore, what would be the condition of that Being which
arose from the consideration of other realities? (Such
form of Being carries no meaning and is absolutely unreal.)

Lamha 3

It should not be imagined that the need of the First is
felt only in the termination of the possible chain of being,
even though the nature of every one possessing the possible nature actualised through the First stands in need
of it. And this to the extent that, if an emanation emanates from the First, and the other emanation emanates
from that emanation, then the other one will stand in
need of only the first emanation, even though that first
emanation stands in need of the First. Nay, it is not so.
The possible nature, when it is actualised in its actuality
or in its essence, stands in need of the First alone, without
any intermediary between the two.

When you attribute anything to the One, its attribution is like the attribution the number one has towards
the cardinal numbers. But by that I mean that one
precedes two and is present in every number, till it
becomes what it is. To God this is the most sublime simile.

Lamha 4

There are two sayings about a thing which is different
from one separated from it. Either we would say "It is It"
or would say "It is not It". In that case, it is a compound,
multiple in itself, preceded by someone else.

The First, therefore, must necessarily be a thing which
may not conflict with other things. For that, we give
examples from matter and external form, even though its
(First's) case is not like any thing.

The existence of wax does not conflict with the existences of images made out of it. Human existence does not
conflict with the existence of human individuals, and the

existence of the faculty does not conflict with the existence of the actions emanating from it. Similarly, every higher existence does not conflict with the lower one, but it is the same thing itself and is also with itself, just as it is in the other thing and is also with it.

The particularisations in no way particularise its reality, and the predications cannot be pronounced on it in particular. Knowledge cannot have connection with it, as it particularises it. It cannot be encompassed by time and place, nor can it be comprehended by the faculty of sense and imagination.

Lamha 5

The First possesses attributes which in fact describe its personal greatness, such as existence, particularisation, life and knowledge. The general rule about them is that when you look at a thing near you and you admire it, then if you seek it in the "first", you will find it (the first) essentially independent of it (the thing), without its acquiring any additional attribute.

The actions of the First are definite and its relations are firm. The general rule about them is that if these actions and relations are to refer to the Invention, then the first emanation suffices all of them; because, considering it as near to the First, its emanation is just the emanation of the whole universe itself. If they refer to the Creation, then the emanation of the Great Body invariably includes all. As the proverb goes "Every kind of game is in the belly of the wild ass".[1]

---

[1] This means that every kind of a game is inferior to the wild ass. It is said to have originated from this fact, that three men went forth to hunt; and one caught a hare; and another, a gazelle; and the third, a wild ass; and the first and the second boasted to the third, who whereupon said as above. It is applied to him who excels his fellows, or to a man who is, with respect to other men, as the wild ass with respect to other kinds of game or to the case of a man who, having several wants, one of which is a great one, accomplishes that great want, and cares not for the others being unaccomplished.

But if they refer to the Administration and the Emanation, then that would be on condition that they (actions
and relations) have either been created by God, or that
He has made a manifestation towards them. Then this
case would be like the case of a sailor in the boat who has
to move if the boat moves, or like the writer, who has
necessarily to move his fingers if he writes.
The First has a peculiar style which defends it against
every form and relation. The rule about them is that
these forms and relations are things which take place in
the brain of the perceptive when his attention, even
though in general drawn towards the greatness of the
First, is also drawn towards one of the forms represented
before him.

Lamha 6

The word one is used in many meanings. Zaid, for example, as an individual is one, though in parts is
multiple. The man in relation to his species is one, though
in relation to individuals is multiple. Similarly, the
animal in relation to the genus (*Jins*) is one, though from
the point of view of species (*Anwa'a*) it is multiple. The
correct meaning of the one, particularly from the point of
view of principle, is that it should come into existence
once from the word "Be", or should come into existence
by one requirement and one power, or be a shadow of
one individual only. Say any of these you like.

Lamha 7

The truth is that only one thing should emanate from
the First; otherwise how can saying "These are two
things" be more proper than saying "These two are
one". Thus it is necessary that their emanation may have
a recourse to two powers, namely, the active and the
passive, which both throw light on the active, and this is
how the whole multiplies.
It is not proper that this emanation should be ex-

clusively attributed to some things rather than others. But it is however necessary that its reality (*Aniyyat*) should not conflict with other realities. Its relation to things is like the relation of the black line to the pictures of writing. We have already given such examples. Thus no other existence can be of that kind except the Self-unfolding One. It is this existence to which allusion is made in our saying "Zaid is in the external world". And it is this same existence hinted at through the word Realities in our saying "Zaid is in the Realities". And it is the same existence pointed out through the word actualisation when we say "Zaid is actualised after he was not". Why should it not be like that, when everything existing in the external and in the Realities is preceded by some thing in the external and in the Realities, and every actualised thing is preceded by its actuality.

Lamha 8

The first thing that comes to your mind is that here is a thing we name Being in the Realities and Being in the external world. And there is a thing in contrast with it we name Not-being.

Sometimes we think of the essence of the Being, and at the same time we doubt the Being of the essence itself, or we declare it (essence) as Not-being. In spite of that, true predications are pronounced on it (essence).

At times we think of the Being but do not think of the essence at all. It is thus, therefore, that your saying "Blackness exists" serves the purpose whereas your saying "Blackness is blackness" does not. While desscribing the essence, you say that this one (essence) exists and that one exists. In both these cases, only one meaning is understood. And from this it becomes clear that the being and the essence are certainly two different things. The meaning of the Being is one which is proved in the essences. But due regard to this problem can be fully paid only when you understand them both thoroughly, and know what they actually are in their essence (*Dhat*, 'zat'). Listen, therefore, to what we say, and content yourself with a summary and not full details.

Lamha 9

What is understood from both sayings, namely, the Being in the external world and the Being in the Realities, is that it is an extraction in thought which has no meaning, save that it is merely represented in your brain. But its extraction is not of the kind that the imagination may invent without relying upon the true reality; but there is its true reality. And if it is there, then your saying "It exists" will be correct and your saying "It does not exist" will be incorrect. If it were not so, namely, that there is no true reality of the Being, then the contrary would be the case. What it is necessary to regard is that reality.

It is not correct at all to say that the case of the reality of Being is like the case of accidents falling upon substances unexpectedly. How could that be? When accidents do not occur unexpectedly when those substances upon which they are to fall unexpectedly are not proved to be in existence. Nor is the case like the case of the matter of the thing, nor like the case of a piece of wax capable of assuming different forms. It is the intellect alone which could make a distinction between them.

The truth is that just as you see both Zaid and 'Amr, you extract man from them. And here the cause of this extraction is proved to exist in both of them. And just as when you see the man and the horse, you extract animal from them. The cause of extraction here is proved in both of them. Similarly, you take notice of all the essences in general, and extract Being from them. The cause of your taking notice is proved in them (essences). Then it is said that the cause of extraction is the thing itself in respect of its being in the external world or in respect of its being in the Realities, just as it is said "Zaid is a man" in respect of the common thing, namely, humanity, between him and 'Amr and Bakr and other human beings.

In reality, Being is the genus of genera and the essence of essences. But the thing is known only by its opposite (*Dhidd*, 'zidd'), while there is no opposite to the nature of Being. It is thus, therefore, that man takes note of things only when he finds differences in the predications (*Ahkam*), which at times are wanting, and at times are present, but there is no difference in the Being in respect of the Being.

The Being, however, cannot be lost sight of in any kind of observation. The conclusion, therefore, arrived at is that it (Being) should not be taken as an essence nor a genus nor any other thing of that kind.

Lamha 10

There is, however, a distinction between every genus and its species and between every essence and its essential. If you were to think it over seriously, you would find that your own perceptive faculty affords you some solution of this problem.

Sometimes you observe all the essences in general and then extract a general existence from them. At times, you observe a particular essence and extract that share of existence from it which is particular to it. General existence is, however, different from particular existence. Thus it is, therefore, that our saying "Blackness exists" serves the purpose while our saying "Blackness is a colour" does not.

Sometimes there are Particularisations (*Taqarrarat*), fixed qualities, in the essence itself or in its necessaries or in its active (*Fa'il*) or passive (*Qabil*). For example, we say that this one is Zaid and that one is Ibn 'Amr. He is a negro, that one is learned, he is a writer and this is a laughing one.

The existence of a thing, however, has been already determined in the higher plane (similitudinary world) before its appearance in its element (material world). And its existence before its flow into its passive element is however in a state of possibility. On that account, it becomes correct for you to extract, in respect of every particularisation, a meaning which you name existence.

In one respect, you find essence existing, but in respect of existence you become careless and begin to say that this essence did not exist before, and has come into existence afterwards. The fact is that the essence has been correctly represented by its existence before you, but you pretend to be forgetful.

Similarly, at times, you apply correct rules to both the absolute unknown and the absolute non-existent. It is so because you in your brain put on them the dress of existence. Thus, if you like, you can say existent in place of absolute non-existent and known in place of unknown. They will then both disclose to you true knowledge, but you again pretend to be forgetful.

Lamha 11

There are forms and accidents in the world, which (accidents) are entangled with them. Besides, therein are matters (without forms) which are a locus for the forms in essence, and a locus for accidents in consequence.

The form, however, goes on advancing towards the higher form, and all forms are an explanation and the details of it. Accidents are advancing towards a general predication, and all the predications are the extension of a circle. The advancement of matters is made towards an absolute matter, and all matters particularise it.

The general form which penetrates absolute matters and preserves the general predication is one body, and a shadow in one respect. Whatever, therefore, may be found in this body, it will have the predication like that of the "Being in the Realities" (*Fi'l Ayan*) or "for the Realities". It is not proper to describe a thing which is higher than that, as "Being in the Realities" or "for the Realities", but by way of convenience. He who desires to put a common factor between the High and the low under the name of being or sight or hearing or power and the like, then he is certainly transgressing.

Yes, the reason also needs some relief when the problem defies solution. Even in the Law there are permissions based on the weakness of the believers. And the relief of reason is to describe the First as the being. Permission is given by the Law to say "God is above the throne, and that He has ears, eyes, hands, shows anger and mercy, and that He is the Hearing and the Seeing".

Lamha 12

A thing is established either by itself or from itself, without standing in need of anyone else or of being established for someone else and standing in need of it. The former is the Self-existent (Being Whose existence is self-necessitated), while the latter is possible.

A thing, the creation and the actuality of which are the outcome of creation and actualisation by the Self-existent, is preceded by a perfection and a requirement. These perfections and requirements, say what you like, are the origins of the emanation of these (created) things. Every perfection requires a particular thing and everything depends on a particular perfection. These perfections and those things are one, save that these perfections are from the necessaries and the relations of the Self-existent, while those things are its information emanating from It. Thus, the whole universe is wrapped up in perfections. The perfections again are disclosed through it. The First does not leave anything little or great but has taken account of it by its sheer essence. Similar is the case of the Great Body in relation to its contents. Here we are giving a simile for this involution and evolution.

Lamha 13

Is it not a fact, that a mathematician when he desires can bring the cardinal numbers into his imagination? Thus, he derives from one, one and one by his reconsideration, and this is how two takes place. Again when he derives from it one and one and one by the repetition of his reconsideration, three is formed. In this way, he derives one number after another, and this is how the units and tens, hundreds and thousands are made. He then joins some of them with others according to the strength of his reason with the result that infinite numbers are formed. He, however, does not make the even odd, or the odd even. Neither does he put a thing in the beginning nor at the end, but he keeps them intact according to the requirement of their numerical nature. From this he does not make any departure nor can he do so.

Now let us take this chain which we have invented as a mirror for knowing the case of numerical nature and its inclusion in the one. From this it becomes clear that this numerical chain implies a hidden secret in the one, so that it (the one) may agree with it (numerical chain) in all its parts. That hidden chain continues to spread over in the field of hypothesis and supposition stage after stage infinitely. Every stage of the number is specified by its properties, and is distinguished by its essence and predications. This spread of the chain is appropriate and restrictive, and is infinite in regard to the comprehension of the mathematician and finite in regard to the one. It is so because the number is derived from the numerical chain included in the one and not from anything else. Every stage of the number is derived from a particular derivation. A number, the emanation of which from the one is possible, emanates without any effort, and that which does not emanate, then it is impossible for it to emanate. From whatever point the derivation may take place, the number derived from it will unavoidably follow from it. These are all the points of its (derivation's) restriction and finity in a certain way.

The number, therefore, has two perfections. The outward, according to the intellectual realisation and the permanency of the mind of the mathematician, and an inward perfection, according to the possibility, the permanency and the virtual senses of the one.

Lamha 14

The things before you, which you see and hear, are the (existing) bodies in themselves. You may find here bodies agreeing with each other in the whole of reality, but differing only in individuality and in its consequences. You may also find bodies which disagree with each other in the whole of reality, but agree in part of reality.

You may, for example, represent the human form to yourself, meditate upon its condition and the condition of the individuals which were united with it, and had already taken place in that you will find that all the individuals are capable of the existence of the human form; and that the human form, with its essentials, potentialities, effects and attributes, is something specified under the limits of its own essence; and its functions and limits are duly fixed.

If the human form is found in matter collected in the womb of such a woman, on such a day, in such a land and with such a mixture, then that will be Zaid. And if it is found in some other matter, on such a day, in such a land, and with such a mixture, then that will be 'Amr, and so on. It is so because human nature comprises in its unity all the individuals in respect of its being a man, and not in respect of its being Zaid, or 'Amr or Bakr. What is meant by it is that the man is the essential of that human nature, while being Zaid or 'Amr are simply the states which occur in the man by accident.

Humanity is like the substance (*Jawhar*), and the states are like the accidents which occur at some times and at other times do not. The individuals and all their predications are implied in humanity and in its predications, in the sense that they are in conformity with the substance, which (substance) requires a straight stature, a constitution and a calling.

For example, if Zaid is found with a certain stature, red in colour, comely in face, and with eyes black and wide, then he will be fitting in with those predications. And if 'Amr is found with another stature, black in colour, ugly in face and with contracted eyes, then he also will be found fitting in with those predications. Similarly, all the items of the predications of the individuals are simply an explanation and the details of the predications of the species.

Then, it is for you to shift from the human species to animality, where humanity and horseity, etc., unite. It also has its fixed limits and its necessary duties to perform. There you reckon all that distinguishes man, where he and the animal differ from each other completely, as an explanation and the details of the predications of animality.

You then shift step by step till you reach the material form which takes in the whole world of matter and its predications. Consequently, this investigation brings us to the conclusion that the whole universe is a necessary thing in the absolute form and its absolute predication; and that the universe is a chain spread out like the spread of the hidden chain in the one.

Still the question arises that the universal even though particularised in a thousand forms does not become an individual; then whence came the individuality? Well, its origin is the Prime matter (*Alhayula alawali*), as it is just like the body for the spirit of the form or like the nest for the bird. The matters then multiplied according to the conditions, because every preceding condition is preparatory for the succeeding one, and thus they required individualities accordingly.

Lamha 15

One quiddity precedes the other due to the paucity of conditions (found in the latter), and because of the mastery one growth asserts over the other. There is a growth which does not come into existence except after the emanation of the elements and the heavenly powers. Their mixture is like the three kingdoms of nature (as they are made of the four elements).

There is a quiddity which comes into creation only

when the common is particularised, like man in relation to the vegetable and so on. There is also a quiddity the proper perfection of which rests on some other thing, like everyday happenings in relation to the Holy Fold, the Sublime Assembly and the Similitudinary World.

Lamha 16

The whole Universe is one body, always changing in its states and everlastingly moving with modal motion. It is so because, even though the forms which particularise the bodily form are the substances themselves, in all the states they become separate (*Mufariqat*) qualities and states for some time in relation to the permanent reality. All the states are revolving. No sooner do they complete the last turn than they begin the first one. Time is included in the permanent and is its requirement, while the power which bears it is Universal Nature. It makes its requirement in the Universal Expediency, only when it is regarded as the Origin of the origin; and by that is meant the (Divine) Providence.

If you go deep, you will not find any cause whatsoever for many existing things except Universal Nature, (Universal) Expediency and Providence. As for example the heat of fire and the coldness of water, the first being particularised with polarity and the second being particularised with movement. The bearer of all these things, assuming different modes of entity, is the Great Body, the hidden container. All are restricted to it, one by one.

Lamha 17

I have come to know that there is a bird with a long neck in the farthest part of India. Its species is confined to one bird named Qaqnus. It always goes on moving from one district to another, and changing from one state to another till it becomes very young. At that time, love stirs within its heart and it begins to sing like the singer. It is then so much moved by the song that it continues to sing more and more, till it is taken over by a state of burning. It dies and becomes reduced to ashes. The spring rain then falls upon it and lo! another bird is created from it through the creation of a worm. This phenomenon continues *ad infinitum*.

Lamha 18

Some people think that the proof of agreement invalidates this kind of succession,[1] but in my opinion this is a sophism. It is so because to take a possible case for granted, does not lead to the impossibility of having knowledge of it, (particularly) when there may be no contradiction and contrast of any kind between them. If there is any contradiction or contrast between them, then that will surely lead to the impossibility of having the knowledge of it. Here one of its sides is infinite while the other is finite with a known beginning. And infinity is contradictory to both the decrease and the increase.

When you take both of them (the decrease and the increase) as infinite for granted, impossibility will follow, because of taking the two contraries together for granted at one and the same time. But when you take them as finite for granted, for which the continuation of one without any agreement is necessary, impossibility will not follow.

Lamha 19

If you take existence in the Realities to mean that it is acquired in this body after the penetration of the form into matter, then it will not be correct to take only the form or only the matter as "existing in the Realities". However, you can take existence to mean that it is acquired in the whole of this body, and then take them both as existing.

But the most correct view is that there is one existent, not duality. Duality has also its own aspect.

[1] The reference is to the rebirth of Qaqnus.

Time is the (name of) measure of motion and change, whether the motion be positional or modal, as the nature of sound may predicate. The origin of time is this body, capable of undergoing changes infinitely. Thus, if a man says that "time" is a substance, you may not deny it completely and take this same body as "place". And if he says that "space" (free from matter) is a substance, you should also not deny that completely.

Lamha 20

When this (particular) body becomes free from all forms excepting one, and if afterwards a certain form takes place, then if one were to ask why it (the form) did not happen before and has happened now, or if he were to ask, why one who is free from change (God) has chosen a particular time for its (the form's) origination?

The answer is this. The one free from change has originated the body which is permanent (*Baqi*). It has also originated a nature in it which manages and rules it well. It has also originated a hidden chain in nature, which happens to be its predication, and the body has to go by it necessarily. This whole system of the body is not subject to any change whatsoever. That nature, on account of its hidden predication, does not leave the body alone. It acquires a form in it one after another, till a certain "state" becomes complete. Every preceding form is preparatory to the succeeding one, and all these combined together prepare for the appearance of (its) decomposition. Every decomposition is the preparatory to what it is made of, till there may remain so much that the one may be without any represented form. This is just like the ball, one turn of which is preparatory to another turn, and every preceding part of the movement is preparatory to its succeeding part. Or it is just like the root of a tree, in the nature of which was ingrained at the very beginning of its creation that it will grow, will reach its vigour of life, then will start decaying until it will be finally reduced to nothingness.

Lamha 21

It is necessary for the grace of God and His wisdom that the first thing to emanate from Him should be the One, the Intellectual and that (One Intellectual) in essence is the Great Body divested of the accompaniments of matter. It is so because the Universe in relation to its Creator is not like the building in relation to its builder, who did some work in the mud and then his work stopped; or if he dies or shifts to some other place, the building will remain intact. It is not so. But its example is like that of the sun, which illumines the earth with its light, and its illumination does not cease from spreading the light even for a moment unless a barrier comes between it and the earth.

The work of the Creator of the forms is firstly to create the origin, namely the Great Body, which is composed of two powers, active and passive. Secondly, to create all those things which are ingrained in the Great Body's nature. And thirdly, to preserve all those things as long as it survives. Thus, the extent of emanation from It would be to illumine this one time and to illumine that other time. Its continuous emanation from the First is, however, necessary for its own continuation. This is what becomes the Great Body. When its time comes, it becomes one of the created beings.

If you were to incline to the side of the Real (God), you would find that it does not emanate from It, and this same Great Body is (always) there with It. Everything attributed as having been emanated from the Real is, in fact, attributed to the Great Body, because of the latter's being mingled with the former. And if you were to turn from the side of the Real, you would again find that the Great Body and nothing else emanates from It, and this same Great Body is (always) there with It, and this same one is the Universal Soul (*An Nafs al-Kulliyat*).

He who believes that the Great Body is the first emanation is right, save that he preferred a summary. And he who believes, that the first emanation is the "Intellect" is also right, save that he made investigation and was rightly guided. It is thus that the Real encompasses all actions done by the Great Body, excepting neither great nor small. Some people, however, have engaged themselves in the search for the cause of the movements of the celestial spheres, and this search has eventually led them to bodies included in the unity of the Intellect, but they overlooked other bodies which were there. Some understood their tremendous multiplicity but failed to understand that unity which embraces multiplicity. "People, however, follow the line they love" is a well-known saying.

Is it not a fact that the "even" has four relations?

(1) When you say that this "even" is such, and thereby you mean the number "four", the "even" in this case is the name of the number "four", so mixed up with it that due to the close mixture, it is not possible to make one accord with the other. The number "four" in its essential stage is not the "four", as long as it is "even" there, and is not "even". But the four is "four" in the sense that, if you were to seriously consider the perfection of its essence, it (four) will be "even" and nothing else. In all the relations, this consideration elucidates the actual case better, and is much more explanatory of the way of its (even's) emanation from it (four) and its revival by it.

(2) You take into consideration this compact mixture, and say that, "four" are "even", and you thereby happen to take that meaning of "even" which is correctly applicable to the number "four", while there is a separation between the two in one respect and a mixture in the other respect. Then, if you were to look at both respects, it will be found correct to make one of them accord with the other. And the meaning of your saying will be that though "four" and "even" are two established meanings in this stage, they are both united in a stage we imagine here in this descent in general. It is just like your saying "Min" (from) is a particle and a conjunction in our saying "I travelled from Basra". Here, when its (Min's) being a particle and a conjunction is taken into con-

18

sideration, you ask whether that "Min" is a particle and a conjunction, and say that this "Min" inclines to the conjunction, becomes free from its being a particle and turns out to be a noun.

(3) When you take this definition into consideration and make a certain analysis of it, and say that "even" by which is meant the adjective "four" stands for four, you thereby happen to have changed "even" from the line of reality, and have taken something (even) which requires that kind of division which exists in the number "four", divided it (number) into two things, and have not taken that thing in the sense the number "four" in particular requires. You have implied the separation which was concealed in it in the stage of definition but have manifested it, and you have implied the mixture which was manifest there, but have concealed it.

At times, on the other hand, the other term is derived, that is its state of being "even", and you say that the state of being "even" is an adjective of "four", stands for it, is present for it and is established in it.

(4) You take into consideration the stage of the adjective, namely, that "four" is "even", and regard this adjective "even" as standing for "four" and established in it, then seek the relation between them, and say that the first (four) is a cause and the second (even) is its effect. The first is the origin, the source, and the second is an emanation and an origination.

If you want to seek the farthest goal in ascertaining the truth, then you should know that the first emanation is the name of the First of the first and is its frontispiece. But, if you are unable to go so far and deep, then better come down to some other stage.

Lamha 22

When the world becomes ready to receive a celestial form or an elemental form or a mineral soul or a vegetable soul or an animal soul or a human soul, that form or soul overflows (towards the world). Or if a certain place necessitates the existence of a form, that place is joined to it.

The reality of this overflow is that the Universal Soul is the sustainer of matter. When matter assumes the form of its sustenance which descends and goes to sustain it, or if the reverse be the case (irrespective of the preparation of the world), then the Universal Soul may appear as a whole in some other form, just as humanity appears both in this particular person and in that particular person.

The reality of this sustenance is that the soul after its penetration into matter gives rise to its predications, such as individuality and limitedness. Whenever matter assumes a certain shape, its general predication descends towards a particular one. The animal soul, for example, after its penetration into the body occasions a particular constitution and the general consequences. Similarly, when the human soul penetrates into the body, it (body) is also particularised by the particular constitution and the consequences.

This is the predication of man and other beings. All that appeared from the Universal Soul and matter time after time was, in fact, already included in them.

Lamha 23

The reality of appearance (*Dhuhur*) in the external world is that one thing should be of such oneness as may suit a certain condition, and it may be dressed in the accidental forms which fall upon it unexpectedly, even though they in their essence may be substances one after another. It is in this way that this may become that all, and that all may become this. But this, however, should not be by way of distribution and division. When a thing in its very essence is not particularised in the particularisation and oneness by which it stands, and then you conceive of a form that follows it, and consider this condition before the appearance of the First in this manifestation, you will find the apparent permanent in its particularisation, its existence and in its oneness throughout the changes; it is most sublime and subtle, while the particularisation, the existence and the oneness maintain the manifestations.

Whenever the thing happens to be an essential part in the manifestation, one manifestation separates from the other, as it is then a separate accident in relation to the apparent, like the man, the horse and the animal in relation to their bodily forms and individuals.

The species of man, for example, is apparent in many human bodies. No human body will be found anywhere but that the human species will apply its rule to it, which is "La Bi Shartin". The multiplicity that came in the manifestation (*Mazahir*, Phenomena) from the side of matter, does not in any way clash with the oneness of the apparent. The oneness is, however, quite safe and secure against all conditions. This is a kind of appearance.

An analogy is that of wax. When it is made in the form of a square on one occasion, the consequences of the square will emanate from it. And when it is made in the shape of a hexagon at another time, the consequences of a hexagon will emanate from it. The waxen existence remains the same throughout, while the existence of a square and a hexagon is appearing and disappearing. This also is a kind of appearance.

Another example is that of a faculty in relation to its actions. Knowledge, for example, is a faculty existing in the mind of the learned. Likewise, smithcraft and carpentry remain unchanged in spite of the change of actions. This faculty has been in the learned from long ago, and it is a firmly-rooted quality which the (human) soul has accepted and is duly coloured by. The learned, after he has acquired it, does not depend upon any particular attention (for its retention). When he pays attention to a particular thing, its picture gets engraved on the tablet of his brain. It is the human soul that gains mastery over the thing through that faculty, as the faculty is a medium between the human soul and the engraved picture. Thus it becomes necessary for the faculty to mingle with and penetrate the picture.

When the faculty, after becoming free, comes near the human soul, it finds what had been already ingrained in it (faculty). At that time, you name it "Ilmun Bil Shay Al-fulani". After this, when the faculty shifts to another science, pays attention to it, another picture is engraved on the tablet of your brain; and it (faculty) gets mingled with that picture. That also is called "Ilmun Bi Dhalik Al-shay" and so on. This is also a kind of appearance.

Here is one more example. The number one has the potentiality to turn into half if one is added to it, or can become one third if two more are added to it. It can also turn into one fourth if three are added to it. Thus, in one, all the grades of numbers are included and it (one) itself is always present in every grade. This also is a kind of appearance. You therefore know that appearance is of various kinds, and that there is an inclusion preceding each one of them. Think over this.

Lamha 24

Existence in the Latent Realities (*A'yan thabitat*) is different from existence in the external world, just as there is a difference between the rays of the sun and the rays of the moon. Again, the rays of the moon that fall on the mirror and are afterwards reflected are not like its rays which are reflected after their having fallen on the earth. Or that difference is like the difference which is seen between the whiteness of ice and the whiteness of ivory.

The higher existence is (the name of) the faculties of Divinity. Next to it is Intellectual existence. When you ascend towards Divinity, you will find there a differentiating attribute, which, in truth, is the Divinity itself, and which (attribute) according to Divinity is in the category of non-existence.

Then if you descend towards the Intellect, which after the Divinity is the strongest existence, you will find it, according to the Intellectual existence and because of the perfections of the First Principle, a wide, extensive world, and a commentary on all existences. The Intellect has a consequence which accompanies its condition, just as it is necessary for Zaid to move his fingers when he writes. Or which is found like the existence of time which is there because of the existence of motion or on account of rest which is opposite to it. This consequence is the Universal Soul.

When you incline to the Universal Soul, you will find it settled and established, without an equal and without any rival in its rank. It is unique as here both Being and the Universe are in agreement.

Particular souls are joined to the Universal Soul, and they in relation to their mothers are like the embryos in their (mothers') stomachs when both are mixed with each other. In relation to the human body they are like the members of the body; and the members of the body are the celestial spheres and the elements.

The relation of the three kingdoms of nature (animal, vegetable and mineral) to the celestial spheres and the elements is like the relation that carbuncles, tumours, fever and the headache have to the body of man. The case of the other bodily diseases is also the same. Some of them are simple while some are septic. The relation of the Similtudinary World to the Univeral Soul is like the relation the designs have to the imagination of an architect.

There are the kingdoms of nature. If you turn to them, you will find them firmly-rooted in a certain way in their stage. Then, there are accidents entangled with them. These accidents are only the particulars of the general accident. They are entangled with the germinative plant in respect of its being a body, just as these substances are the necessaries for the absolute body: that is, that a body should have a particular shape, a particular quantity and a particular quality (Kaif).

After the accidents, there are two other stages. One is allegorical existence. What pertains to it, is as follows:

(1) To take the indications of a thing as a substitute for an ordinance in the Divine Law. Wine, for example, has an existence other than its substantial one, and this

very wine turns the good into bad in the sense that, if it is taken as a custom, it will spoil the social good, the household good, the good of life and that of civilisation. Thus it is, therefore, that it came as a corruption in allegorical existence.

(2) To take the symbols of writing and verbal sounds in place of their meanings. Thus, divination also came according to this allegory.

(3) To put actions in the place of faculties, the offerings to God in the place of implorations, and invocations to God in the place of their meanings. Consequently, injunction to that effect appeared in the circle of the "Companions of the Right hand".

At times, the Divine causes agree upon occasioning an event, the death of Zaid, for example. Then the prayers of people and their appeals for help rise towards the Sublime Assembly with the result that, in the place of death, it (Sublime Assembly) is satisfied with its (death's) allegorical existence, such as causing some sort of an injury to Zaid or some loss of his valuable property.

The other stage is of those worlds which are formed in the absolute imagination and appear in the mixture of accidents. The reason being that elemental angels and devils, in spite of the fact that they exist by themselves, have wonderful meetings and agreements in the absolute imagination. They leave their effects on human nature through certain movements, ailments and thoughts of men.

Sometimes, one of them (elemental angels and devils) longs to assume a particular human quality with the result that one thing attracts the other. It helps in the thought of it, and is delighted in it, and is named accordingly. In such cases, they use a strange language, and have strange meetings and usages with humanity, which cannot be properly comprehended except by one who has made an exhaustive study of this kind of existence.

Remember, that an existence cannot be known except when it is taken as necessary. The Divinity for example, can be known only through the Divinity, and the Intellect only through the Intellect. Similar is the case of every specific nature which cannot be understood except through that alone. The gnostic, however, understands a thing by means of that thing thoroughly and completely, while the rest of people understand only those things which are strong in the composition of their existence. For example, the majority of people understand only the earthly compounds.

Sublime existence, such as the Universal Soul and the Intellect, cannot be seen by them but from afar, in the form of a phantom. As for the lower existence, like the other two existences, weakness of the soul and scanty wakefulness of the mind are a condition for knowing it. Thus there is some kind of an agreement between the knower and the known. It is thus, therefore, that you see those who are engaged in calling up a Jinn, by gazing on a drawing of the Jinn, are like tom-fools and children. Similarly, when you see people hearing a gnostic who says "Time is an existent and the world is a phantom", they take him to be a liar and a fool, while as a matter of fact he is perfectly correct in what he says.

Lamha 25

Sometimes, a thing has two existences. One existence happens to be the condition of the other existence. The world, at times, according to the celestial and the elemental powers becomes ready for the overflow of some existence. It has become clear that human existence is an overflow of an existence which is of a stage higher than humanity.

Similarly, at times, it is decided in the sublime Assembly to occasion an event, such as the emergence of a nation or the existence of Zaid or his death or the descent of some calamity on him on such and such day. When the time of his (Zaid's) human existence comes, his spiritual existence mingles with it, as faculty mingles with a particular action.

At times, a thing comes into existence according to the requirement of the agent or because the patient has reached its end, or because the thing happens to be the "maqbul" of some other thing, or that the agent has reached its end.

In short, one thing requires another thing, from the point of view of its being either the agent or the patient. Or it often so happens that, though the patient and the agent are present, the time of existence of the required thing has not come as yet, either because of the absence of a cause or an external condition. Or because of the presence of some obstacle there. For example, an artisan makes a most beautiful and elegant body from wax, which so pleases those who see it that they begin to say, "How beautiful is this, how expert is its artisan".

Now here the presence of a form was absolutely necessary, but that was not there before the artisanship. It was, however, ingrained in the mind of the artisan, as his faculty requires the sequence of actions from him. If, for example, the action of the faculty has connection with this particular place, then this would be the particular idol.

Similarly, the wax is a patient in which the idol appears; because it was already dressed in the original form, namely the colour and the shape. This case at times is made clear by the picture which was already there (before its appearance in the wax), and at times by this actual picture (after its appearance in the wax). The idol even at the very outset seems to combine the waxen predications and those of this picture, but deep thinking discloses two existences in it, whose existence has mingled with the picture of a man, whether the matter from which it is formed is wax or wood or stone. And their existence is the wax itself, whether the picture formed from it is the picture of a man or of a horse or of a tree.

The first existence depends on the agent, and if it is to rest on its (agent's) "renewed attribute", it will continue as long as the agent continues or will continue provided it happens to be ascribed this attribute (of the agent). The second existence depends on the patient and will continue with its continuation or will continue if it is also ascribed its (patient's) attribute. This example, however, falls short in one way, because the agent here is preparing to keep its connection with the thing, while the Agent which is in the universe is a Real Agent, the connection and the permanency of which do not cease.

Thus whenever such an attribute on which it (existence) rests is found, the emanation of that existence would be necessary in the spiritual world. This attribute is nothing but the spiritualities of the celestial spheres and the powers of the elements. Whenever this existence is found, the Sublime Assembly imagines that thing as existing. Accordingly, this existence becomes composed of the celestial powers, the beautiful elemental natures and the similitudinary thoughts. Then that event is found in the world of mortals.

Sometimes the first existence happens to be in a summary form capable of elucidation by the second existence or it is neglected. This same intermingling is in other words the descent of the Iron, the Balance and the Blessing from heaven, about which the Holy Qur'an speaks. This very intermingling is the descent of misfortunes and their remedy through prayer, the descent of countless trials like the fall of rain on the houses of the Arabs, to which reference is made in the sound Tradition.

Lamha 26

Know that the daily happenings which are seen happening from day to day certainly have their complete causes behind them, from which their effects appear unavoidably. If it were not so, then it would mean that this existence had taken place without its necessary complete cause. It is also not possible that it (cause) should be only the eternal, as in that case it would be the eternal and non-temporal. Thus, investigation has forced us to search for what may be connected with the eternal, so that the whole (the connecting link and the eternal) may become a complete cause.

Similarly, intelligent people have always persisted in the search for those complete causes. They observed elemental natures and there they found a basis for them. As the happenings continued to happen repeatedly, hypotheses were made about them, till there remained no doubt in the mind of any one about their causes.

They further observed the movements of the planets and the opposition of some to others, and subsequently found that some planets do influence the objects of sense, like the change of heat and cold by the change of the relation of the sun to the earth or like the change in the location of water; and like the ebb and flow of the tides by the change of the relation of the moon to the earth.

There are some things which in the opinion of a certain section are not objects of sense, but in spite of that others apply themselves exclusively to investigating them and understanding them also. They are shifting from the particulars to the universal which combines them, and are moving towards forming a hypothesis about effects which when joined with others assume the form of a happening, like the change in the character of people and what happens to them with the change of the oppositions of stars.

Then they put such science into writing, by which means the knowledge about them becomes complete: sciences such as astronomy, geometry and the science of the properties of vegetables and animals. After that, those sciences which were their branches and offshoots were put into writing, like the science of witchcraft and of talismans and the science of medicine.

These people were followed by men who were always engaged in searching for the causes of things. They found out a cause for each one of them. And they have mentioned in their books that the circular movement is neither voluntary nor natural, but is the result of a Universal scheme and then of an imaginary one.

The celestial spheres certainly have souls, and they

influence the three kingdoms of nature as our own souls influence some parts of our bodies. By their utmost concentration they seek all wherein lies the good of these three kingdoms. At times, their connection becomes the cause of both the possibility and the impossibility of inspiration. When people plead with them for help and for generosity, they knock at the door of generosity in the same manner as the antecedent leads to the consequent. "And whosoever knocks at the door of the generous, will surely find it open." The celestial spheres cause the raising of the messengers and of the nations, the appearance of miracles and the acceptance of prayers.

Lamha 27

In the opinion of philosophers, the causes of happenings are of two kinds, and they are:

(1) The heavenly powers.
(2) The earthly powers.

The heavenly powers again are of four kinds, and they are as follows:

(1) The passivities of the souls of the heavenly powers which result from the effect of the intellectual principles. The interpretation of these words in my opinion is that the bodily forms become the seat for the (manifestation of) predications. These are the models of the species stripped of matter. They are attributable to the requirement of the Divine essence. This much, however, you know.

(2) The natures of the stars which influence the three kingdoms of nature in various ways. The difference found in their influence is either the result of the situation of these kingdoms surrounded by the stars, which lends support to their properties or protects them from them. Or that difference is the result of the difference of their rays. Thus nothing takes place on the earth but that in which their powers have combined according to their (stars) oppositions. Or this difference is the outcome of

the normal state or otherwise of the radiation of their rays.

The ancients have said that whosoever enters into sexual intercourse while the planet Venus is in the house of Pisces (Zodiacal house), and the Moon happens to be in the sixth phase of its light, and both the inauspicious planets, Saturn and Mars, are also not opposed to it, then such love and harmony will take place between husband and wife that people will begin to wonder. And whosoever enters into sexual intercourse while the planet Venus is burning hot either in the house of Virgo or of Aries, and Mars (the less inauspicious one) is opposite to it (Venus) or is in its fourth receptacle or Saturn (the more inauspicious) is in conjunction with it or is opposite to it, and the planet Jupiter is falling away from it, then that conjunction of theirs will be accompanied by great misfortune. Consequently, such mutual hatred will take place between them that it will strike people with wonder. They have mentioned many a fact of this kind.

(3) The perceptive, the intellectual, the imaginative and the thinking faculties. The chain of created beings accepts them as they are, whether they be in its favour or against. At that time, Divine Providence inspires people to admire their precession. If there is something implied in the chain of created beings, but there is no earthly cause to occasion it, then its cause is also created in the earth. Or if there is a weak cause which is not customarily and usually so effective as to bring about the desired result, then their admiration strengthens that weak cause, till it becomes effective to achieve that desired result. Or if there is a harmful cause, this admiration restrains it to the extent that it ceases to harm. An illustration of this is the expansion God brought in the power of cold in the air which surrounded the fire of Abraham.

Sometimes inspiration influences the hearts of people, and even of animals. If the intention at that time is to bring about the reformation of a great many people, and some person at that time is also found quite alive to it (understands that intention), and there is no other purpose for that person to serve except this, then such a person is named a "prophet".

(4) The powers which imply some sort of a cause for occasioning earthly happenings. And that cause of theirs is not there because of its own effect, but is due to some form of the thing which produces a particular effect, just as you see water is made to serve us by digging watercourses, and the winds by building canals. The nature of water always requires downward flow. If the earth is dug so that the place where it is intended to bring water is at the lowest level, the water by its nature will surely flow in that direction. The same is the case for the winds when they meet with an obstacle that prevents them from following their natural course. Where canals are built to face the winds, the winds by nature will beat on them. And this very opposition makes possible the sailing of boats in the intended direction.

The faculties of the celestial spheres are like the parts and limbs of human beings. Nay, they (the human beings) even know them spiritually. Therefore, when a man humbly supplicates the powers which are dominating him, namely, the faculties of the spirits of the celestial spheres, whether he calls them celestial souls or angelic souls which are free from bodies or anything else, and strengthens his humble supplication, their thoughts and their faculties begin to move towards what he has supplicated for. An example of their admiration for it is similar to what we feel in the presence of food, the satiation and taste which excites our appetite for it. Appetite in exciting the movement of our hands and feet is just like the presentation of the preliminaries for the emergence of a result from the higher principles.

As regards the earthly powers, they are also of four kinds, and they are as follows:

(1) The active powers of nature, which are deposited in the elements and in the simples (substances), and in every specific form in particular. Fire for example warms and water cools.

(2) The passive powers of nature, like the tree which burns, the iron that melts and the stone which neither burns nor melts.

(3) The willing, active powers, like the power of speech in us. Or like the occurrence of weakness in the body, the seizure of mind by fear and shame. Or like the body's becoming red and the rise of anger in the heart, and like the slipping of the foot when one is suddenly struck by fear. Similarly, they influence weak minds, as influences the evil eye.

(4) The willing powers, which are influenced by the heavenly powers or by the earthly souls which are stronger than them (willing powers). On this much at least all the research philosophers are agreed.

(5) The actions of people, as they are their particular causes.

(6) The divine names, which arise from the worshipping devotees and the superior angels. They assume the form of luminous bodies in the Similitudinary World and there the angels obey them. When the Changer (God) turns them by some kind of personal intention towards itself and pulls them to the desired object, they incline towards it, and the angels who are the servants of the Divine names yield to them. God willing, we shall soon make clear some of its rules.

We have observed that there is no contradiction between the heavenly and the earthly powers. But it is necessary for them to have a universal flow, so that all the universals may unite in one form, and the right of each one of them may be duly regarded in the happening taking place. Such an example is seen in the mirror, the person looking and the picture formed in the mirror. Here the necessary point in the mirror and in the person is a universal order which conforms to the picture.

Similarly, there is no contradiction between this order which we held as necessary for both the heavenly and the earthly powers and these causes which we have mentioned. Yes, sometimes one thing happens to be more strongly necessary and the other happens to be its supporter but is not necessary. At times, one thing happens to be more strongly demanding than the other. At that time, the Changer inclines the happening towards the stronger one. The truth is that the causes are reinforcing one another, but it (Changer) desired to give due regard to the right of every rightful one.

Lamha 28

When things come to oppose one another, and the active powers through various ways and means join and mingle with the passive ones, different things take place. Some in the form of essences and substances and others in the shape of actions and states. There is no evil in these things, and by that is meant the existence of a thing without a cause or its non-existence when there is a complete cause for it. Sometimes, there happens to be evil in them in the sense that they oppose one order against the other, just as burning is good in relation to fire, as it is the sign of its perfection and is the complete requirement of its nature, and is an evil in relation to the animal that burns in it.

These evils are as follows:

(1) Those which are near to pure, irresistible evil. That is so because they happen to be contrary to the illustrious order which is liked by the Divine powers.

(2) Those which are near to pure good, which is just like the real state of normalcy in the body of man. That is so because they happen to be in conformity with the illustrious orders liked by the Divine powers, even though they are contrary to some of the weak and dying ones.

(3) Those evils, the perfection of which takes the form of causing injury and disease in the body of man.

If a thing happens to be an evil for both celestial and earthly causes, but the suppression of those causes is not hateful, then the generosity of the most generous (God) requires that they should be suppressed. And if a thing does not weaken the celestial or the earthly cause but the

expansion of its cause is also not hateful, then the generosity of the most generous requires that it should be
expanded. The reason is that just as the inclusive, over-
flowing chain of existence includes these causes, similarly
it includes all other things as well which are created from
them. And just as the Essence requires those very causes,
similarly it requires a revelation, about which God decides when some of the causes combine. An example is
the properties of the stages of numbers which, like the
stages of the numbers themselves, are the very requirement of numerical nature.

God, according to the action He is doing through the
Universal Administrative nature in creation, always holds
the balance in His hand, by which the causes are
weighed, lowered and raised. He knows the preponderant
cause which rules the preponderated. God says "Every
day He is in a new splendour".[1] He gives life and brings
death, lowers and raises. He has said "We have not
created the heaven and the earth and what is between
them in vain, that is the opinion of those who dis-
believe".[2] That is, (they have been created) useless,
purposeless without any plan and without specifying a
particular thing before bringing it into existence.

He is, therefore, looking after every soul and every
cause, particularising every thing with its required condition. He deals with them by suppression and expansion,
and by inspiring the angels, human minds and even the
animals; and by transforming what is in the world of the
three kingdoms of nature, till the thing returns to the
desired good. This act of His is like the act of a philosopher who, sitting behind the veil, moves the tools and
the instruments, then through their movement he joins
them in such a way that the seers begin to marvel.

It is also not necessary that for giving preponderance
to one over the other, the action of the Universal Administrative nature in creation should need new intentions

---

[1] Surah Rahman, V. 29.
[2] Surah Sad, V. 27.

and changing decisions. Nay, it is not so, but its action is transcendental and far beyond your speculation.

Lamha 29

When water falls on soft ground, its nature weighs all the directions it flows to and all the obstacles preventing it from its natural flow. It will not then be possible for it to flow in any direction except to the lowest level. Nor will it press against anything when there is a ditch for it to flow in. Nor will it break through the hard ground before the soft. Thus, all its actions are already ingrained in the root of the requirement of its nature from which it cannot escape.

For example, when the root of a tree absorbs the matters of its ingredients, then its administrative nature weighs its matter, its thinness, its thickness, its heat, its dampness and all that is necessary for it to bring forth from the tree the branches, the flowers, the fruits and the gums, etc. Then it (administrative nature) distributes the matter in them, according to its own inherent order. However, it is not possible for it to act more freely in the case of leaves than in the case of fruits, but only when the matter disobeys.

When some injurious mixtures take place in the body of man, the human nature looks into them. If their improvement is possible, it improves their cause accordingly, and turns them into the parts of his (man's) body. But if such improvement is not possible, then it takes them out of the body in the form of hæmorrhage of the nose and diarrhœa. And if they, on account of the disobedience of the matter, do not spread and go out of the body, then it drives them out from the interior of his body to his skin, and thus carbuncles take place. But if in spite of that they do not spread and go out, then fever or a particular kind of disease overtakes some member of the body. This is how all natures weigh in the natural balance all those matters that come upon them. No unreasonable preference is given to one over the other.

Lamha 30

The Universal Administrative nature working in creation is entitled to weigh every thing in the balance, lower it or raise it as the case may be. If you really want to know the truth, then remember that all the balances of nature are a part of the Universal balance. One of its immediate requirements is the happenings resulting from the impossibility of a vacuum, like the breaking of a glass bottle when it is thoroughly squeezed, and like the rising of water in an immersed pipe. If no air intervenes, water will go on rising. All this is from the requirement of the Universal nature which like one thing pervades and penetrates everything. The only difference is that the nature of a thing near to the Prime Origin would be its intention itself, and its intention would be its nature itself.

It is so because, when it (one near the Prime Origin) intends a thing, its intention happens to be eternal, and arises from Universal expediency. This inclusive chain of creation is technically called "Predestination". Then the predications of the Universal nature which appear in the world time after time are termed "Executions".

Lamha 31

It has been proved before us through veridical vision that there is a spiritual plane in existence, which is the origin of many happenings, such as the raising of the prophets and the establishment of new nations. Ancestors have named it the "Holy Fold". We have in it an excellent example to follow.

Now, if you want to understand the reality of the "Holy Fold" thoroughly well, then know that there are many points in every particular soul, and every point has its own particular attributes and characteristics. These points have an origin which necessitates them. The case of these points at the very outset appears to be confusing; but deep thinking which pays due regard to every rightful point does not mix up one thing with another. For example, the human individual is a speaking, walking, laughing, writing and white one, etc., but the point by which he is a white one is not the same by which he is a speaking one. When you see every man as speaking, you are led to the conclusion that the point which makes speech necessary is common in all human individuals. But we find that there is many a stone which is white and many a man who is black. Thus, this point is other than the one by which he speaks, even though they both, the stone and the man, have met together by coincidence at one and the same place. The Universal Soul (like the particular one) has so many points corresponding to every state which is to come upon it one day in life. One of its points corresponds to "establishment" and "actuality". This point is the very image of the "Being" Whose existence is necessary. It is Its manifestation and Its exact copy. This is the origin of the "Holy Fold".

When the celestial spheres came into existence with their knowledge and faculties, the first thing they imagined was the being whose existence was necessary. His form was such that all their knowledge agreed on it. And since there is neither any ignorance nor any kind of confusion, it became necessary that that form of the being should tally with those points to a certain extent. This is the first appearance of the "Holy Fold".

Thereafter, when the causes required that the superior angels and the knowing minds joined with them be brought into existence, they were compelled by their nature to incline to this "Holy Fold" as every creature inclines to its object of inclination. Again, when these angels and the knowing minds reached that point, gathered round it and submissively humbled themselves before it, they acquired certain attributes according to their capabilities. Consequently, the circle of the "Holy Fold" became enlarged. This "Holy Fold", even though it has no particular place from the point of view of location, the nearest interpretation of it is that it is the

"Rahman" sitting on the Throne.[1] The angels of high rank are bearing that Throne, and it is from here that the Execution proceeds.

Lamha 32

Just as the vegetable body has a nature which includes the whole of its system, similarly the Universal Soul has also a nature which includes the system of the whole creation. The celestial spheres and the elements are formed in it. When they mingle with each other they give rise to the three kingdoms of nature. Again, when these kingdoms came into opposition, they occasioned states some of which were near to the "relative good" and some far away from it. It, however, always becomes necessary for the Divine grace to promote the cause of good as far as it may be possible. On this analogy, some things depend and rest on others. According to the complete cause, there is neither any disagreement nor any agreement in those consequences, neither the expansion of an action nor its abandonment. But there is a continuous chain, and the nature does not digress a bit from it. Then that inclusive chain appears set on that line from which it does not divert.

As the Universal Soul and its nature flow from the First and continue by its continuation, it became necessary that the Universal nature should rest on that part which resembles the First, and on the point which among all its points is nearest to the First. That shining point by its light has dominated all that is in creation, and by its effectiveness has penetrated every object of the phenomena. All that we have attributed to the Universal nature issues from it. Accordingly, he who has seen that point and has observed its domination, would say in reply to this question of the questioner "Where was our

---

[1] By "Rahman" in the philosophy of Shah Waliyullah is meant the manifestation of the person of God on the Throne in the same manner as the human form is reflected in the mirror.

38

Lord before He created this creation"? that "He was in a dark cloud, above and below which was no air".[1]

The relation of the Universal point by virtue of its being in the dark cloud descends before it gets branched off in species and genera, even though a new intention may be proved for God which may become the cause of happenings. But that intention of His needs no recourse whatsoever to anything else, just as fire for its being a "burning one" needs no cause other than the fiery nature, or just as the Execution which descends, rests upon the Throne. And he (the answerer to the questioner) in his reply should say that the angels become obedient to it (descending Execution).

Lamha 33

The works of God are very many, but they do not exceed the following four kinds:

  (1) Invention (*Ibda'a*)
  (2) Creation (*Khalq*)
  (3) Administration (*Tadbir*)
  (4) Emanation (*Tadalli*)

  (1) Invention means to bring out a thing from pure non-existence into existence. This work is (continuing) between God and that which changes from state to state. What necessitates it (the invention) is the possibility and the thing's being not necessary by its existence. Its origin is the necessity and the need.

  (2) By creation is meant making a thing from a thing (as the making of Adam from dust). This is between God and what passes from one state to another state. The consequence that results from it is the appearance of the celestial spheres, the elements and other species with their properties and effects. What necessitates it (the creation) is that the created thing should be preceded by its matter and some passage of time, and that the Universal Soul should be inclusive of all things.

[1] A reference to the Tradition.

When some powers mix with other powers, their mixture requires that the Universal Soul should descend upon this portion of the body in due proportion. Their origin is the appearance of what was concealed, and an existing thing's dressing itself in the garment of other existence. The agent of it is the Divine Essence, as it makes a continuous flow towards the Universal Soul, which by its properties and predications is capable of receiving that flow.

(3) As regards Administration, it refers to the free acting in the universe so that the happenings therein should turn in conformity with the Universal Expediency. This (work) is between God and those things which are a place of multiplicity, like the species and the individuals. What necessitates it (the administration) is the inter-mixture of powers. Had there been no Administration, that intermixture would have led to evil, which it was necessary in the wisdom of God to reject. Its origin is the inspiration with which beings possessing the power of will are inspired, such as the angels, men and animals. And also its origin is the transformation of the natures of the three kingdoms and the creation of causes composed of both the inspiration and the transformation. The agent here is the Divine Essence, under the condition that it acts in the soul by way of creating species and genera, and provided that it (Divine Essence) takes into consideration both the Universal Expediency and the one which accepts the three kingdoms of nature.

(4) Emanation originally means the appearance of the Real (God) as an Administrator in the world in the same manner as the human soul is the administrator of the body. The appearance of the reflection of this Emanation in dreams or in wakefulness or in the hereafter is the result of it (appearance of God). The first kind of appear-ance is the source of Administration in the world, while the second kind of appearance is between God and human individuals. The appearance of knowledge, of guidance and of the perfection of the selves is the result of it. What necessitates it (Emanation) is that religions may

be prescribed for the people and their perfection may be achieved through the Universal Expediency, which cannot become complete on that day but by Emanation. The agent of this Emanation is God, provided He is characterised by the Administration, and the whole of human species and human beings accept that Emanation.

Lamha 34

Creation is the completion of Invention, and Administration is the completion of Creation, while Emanation is the completion of Administration. It is so because by Creation is meant free action both in the matter and in the form, which gives rise to the multiplicity of forms. All this is (primarily) included in the Universal Soul and the Universal Matter. When Creation appeared, it was nothing save a mixture of powers and an appearance of the contents of the Universal Soul and the Universal Matter.

When God made the first invention, He summarily poured into it all that will continue to appear from it everlastingly. Again, when the species and the individuals appeared with all their effects and predications, and pressed one against another, the Universal Nature weighed them all, and gave preponderance to the Universal Expediency which originates from the very root of it (Universal Nature).

Administration is solely concerned with the creation of knowledge, intentions, transformation of natures (of the three kingdoms) and the preparation of able persons for bearing the Legal responsibility. It ultimately ends where the reflection and the manifestation of the Great Manifestation appear in the Holy Fold. The Nature of existence requires that what has been strengthened by Creation should not be done away with by Administration and what has been strengthened by Administration should not be done away with by Emanation.

Administration, however, will not do away with the species of devils and the spirits which are always commanding the doing of evil. For that, the angels and the prophets will be sent who will work against their activities.

Lamha 35

The main cause which is to be taken into consideration in the universe is Universal Expediency. The procession of things from the Origin by way of necessity is due to the requirement of their causes. In our opinion, there is no clash if they proceed through the necessary intention or through the requirement of causes. Just as there is a power in a vegetable body which is the origin of transforming the food into what suits the body, and there is a power which is the origin of growing leaves, flowers, branches and fruits in a particular way, and there is a power which is the origin of an appointed time in which the vegetable body grows to a known limit, stays on, withers and dries, and its effects profit and benefit. Similarly, there is a Universal Nature in the Great Body which requires that the members of the body should be of this kind, and that every species and every thing should be such-and-such. Then that thing does not differ in any way.

If two causes disagree with each other in one and the same matter, then it is necessary that the decision should be such-and-such. When the cause of the "great good" may be found missing, and its creation according to the Universal order included in the Universal Nature may not be unfavourable, then it becomes necessary that a remote cause be expanded to some extent so that it may prove useful, and the whole thing may come back to the "great good".

The beginnings and the ends are sometimes attributed to the revolutions of time. And it is said that they (revolutions) influence them. But there is a compliance in this saying. The plain truth is that the beginnings and the ends are attributed to the neighbourhood of the Universal Nature, in which they were once included and then afterwards spread out. But because to understand the Origin was extremely difficult, the philosophers descended from it towards time, but the truth is not hidden from those who know it well.

Lamha 36

The natures of the celestial spheres are also the causes which are to be taken into consideration both in the Creation and in the Administration. The reason being that the creation of the three kingdoms of nature does not take place unless the creative powers unite. Again, in specifying the created being, the condition of the creative powers is to be taken into account.

When the sperm drops into the womb and undergoes many a trial, it becomes a clot of congealed blood, then a lump of flesh, first incomplete and later complete in make-up, ready for the creation of pure air in it, which bears resemblance to spiritualities. When that pure air is created, the Universal Soul descends there in the form of a particular one, suitable to the form of the world that day.

The reason is that when you consider the Rational Soul in both its active and passive aspects, it is found like a ball, the end of the lower point of which is the origin of its (Rational Soul's) parents, and the upper point of which is that from which spreads its origin in the people and in their accepting its grace. These aspects will be succeeded only by what the world on that day requires.

When Fortune happens to include a man of wild nature, it becomes necessary that he may be created with a strong self, so that he may overcome his adversary, and his adversary may not be able to oppose him. Thus all the aspects of the self are created according to the requirement of the form of the world. These aspects of the self are called "Luck". When a child becomes grown-up, and the time of his dealing with his adversary comes, God takes into consideration the condition of his luck. Then no one gets excited to quarrel with him, except one about whom He knows that he would be defeated in his argument by him (the lucky man). Accordingly, God occasions such causes by which he overcomes. In short, He considers the case of this grown-up person according to the requirement of his luck, and the case of all others he has to deal with according to the requirement of their luck, never allowing Expediency to be lost sight of.

The aspects are, however, created in the self when the Rational Soul begins to appear in the foetus. The Holy Prophet, the true and the trusted has informed us that at the time of breathing the soul into the body, four things are written by the order of God: whether he will be a male or a female, unhappy or happy, his deeds and his subsistence. The time the sperm is dropped is the time of the first stage and the time the child is born is the proof of His action. In like manner, in the creation of conditions and in giving practical shape to them, He takes into account the case of the stars. If the conditions require war or peace, God decides that accordingly, and prepares the suitable causes for everything.

Lamha 37

As far as the planet Saturn is concerned, its nature in relation to earth and water requires hatred towards them. Then no disease ever overtakes them which may take them out from their nature to the nature of the three kingdoms. It bears an attribution to the Eternal (God) Who transcends every form. Had it not been so, the signs of God would not have been venerated, and nothing from the three kingdoms of nature would have been attributed to Him.

The planet Mars is a treasury of violence and war, which both excite heat and the burning of nature.

Jupiter in its relation to the three kingdoms of nature is a sign of beneficence. The meaning that flows from it is that the predication of every specific form of the three kingdoms of nature should appear properly. For example, the human form, if it appears in the body at a time when

Jupiter is in power, its predication requires that he should appear full and perfect.

The predication of the Sun on the other hand calls for prevalence. It implies the meaning of worship and attention to the moons of heaven and earth with veneration.

The planet Venus is the source of the flow of all which goes to complete the form. For example, when the human specific form becomes complete in man, he turns out comely and handsome. Similarly, it (Venus) is a proof of the soul in the respect that it comes to bear resemblance to the Divine world, and gets dyed by its dye. It is thus that every gnostic has a share of it.

To the planet Mercury belong the systematised sciences put into writing, and the attention which brings one to it is similar to what the waking one finds at the time of his wakening when he jumps out of his bed and feels the pinch of wakefulness.

The predication of the Moon is the tolerable relation. It (relation) implies a quality of purity. The qualities of these stars are found in every Rational Soul in many respects. But the prevalence and the subjugation are, however, the result of the predication of the conjunctions of the stars, taking place at the time of breathing the soul into the body and the descent of the celestial soul upon it.

Lamha 38

The word "angel" is used in many meanings with regard to different realities. They (meanings) relate to the effects and the properties and not to the spiritual qualities. It is thus, therefore, that the Universal souls with which the predications of the Creation and the Administration are connected, are called "angels". The overflow of beneficence and the knowledge of these angels resemble the nature; as there is neither any new intention in them nor any change, nor any kind of transformation from one state to another state. The human minds, however, reach and join them through their concentration and knowledge and become like them. Consequently, the faculties of those souls make a natural representation to them (human minds), and that becomes the cause of the representation in the Universal wisdom. Similarly, the daily happenings also represent many of their sciences.

Lamha 39

Know that the celestial soul has some kind of a perception for knowing both the past and the future. The reason is that during the time of its perception in its mind, it gains from its Lord (God) a perception of the daily happenings set in order, and also the perception of their causes.

The causes of happenings are either natural, which the celestial souls perceive as one of us perceives what happens to his body. Or they are voluntary, which arise from the celestial souls and reach a natural or a Divine cause, which was made to flow for the sake of "good" on that day. For a flow like this, the powers of the celestial spheres are mostly taken into account. The reason is that the celestial souls are the nearest realities on which the knowledge of the past and the future flows from their Lord.

The strongest of the celestial spheres is the soul of the Crystalline sphere. It dominates all the spheres below it, as you see it dominating them in the daily movement from east to west. Then this perception of past happenings and of those which are to happen in the future is gained by the rest of the spheres and the superior souls joined to them.

The perception of the souls can be like an intellectual perception, but absolute intellectual perception when it happens to encompass all the aspects of the thing, happens to be very near to the particular perception of the "person". Subsequently, when the inferior souls join the celestial ones, thinking and imagination take place. The celestial souls then, on account of a general relation they have with the inferior souls, openly strengthen that thinking and imagination.

In short, when the world is disposed to receive the flow of knowledge, it takes notice of it. That happens in this way. When a particular age is found, and the things corresponding to it are created and the knowledge is changed into what suits them, then a form takes place in your perceptive faculties. The other perceptive faculties then begin to help each other in imagining that form. The form (caught into imagination) at that time stands suspended in the air before its Lord, neither staying on any particular object nor on any particular soul. At that time, it is called a "Similitudinary form". Its predications for the world are as follows:

(1) No happening on earth ever takes place in it unless it has first been found existing in this Similitudinary World for some time. The general existence (of a happening), by which is meant the Writing in the Divine Tablet, may be nearly fifty thousand years prior to its appearance in the Similitudinary World. The detailed existence of important events is of nearly one thousand years, and by that is meant, the "Existence of the souls before their bodies". Every event has, however, a soul which suits it well. When the time of its happening comes, God decides from above the Throne. The angels obey His word, and that event then descends to the earth.

(2) Sometimes, the Divine souls attract an existence or an emanation towards themselves at a particular place with the result that water assumes the colour of an absolute body, and then an existence takes place which does not accept any rend and mend. Such examples are seen in the fire of the prophet Moses, and in the appearance of the angel Gabriel in the form of a well-built human being before Mary. And also in his (Gabriel's) coming to the Holy Prophet in the shape of a questioner to question him about Faith, Beneficence, Islam and the Signs of Resurrection.

(3) The appearance of Paradise and Hell.

Their source is below the Throne where its faculties mix with the celestial faculties. The place of their appearance is sometimes a piece of land, as they once appeared to the Holy Prophet in the niche, while he was offering the Eclipse prayer. Here no person has any right to say that Paradise and Hell appeared only in that form, as the form does not give out heat and refreshing breeze.

(4) There is a kind of angels in whose hearts the inspirations, the imitations and the examples of the World of Similitude are poured according to their capabilities. They are also inspired to pray for mankind. That becomes one of the causes for the flow of the Divine grace. At times, they become able to take the shape they desire. That happens in this way, that their imagination of fear is extraordinarily strengthened by the Similitudinary faculty.

(5) The eye of the seer may fall upon his desired object.

(6) Sometimes water, through the Similitudinary body is turned into an absolute body. Its soul happens to be this "person", and its body, the similitudinary representation.

Lamha 40

Similarly, the name of angel is applied to the souls whose creation the order (Nazm) of the Universal Nature has made necessary. It is so because just as it (order of the Universal Nature) requires the emanation of the species and the universal bodies from the celestial spheres, the elements and the stars, similarly it requires the emanation of the individuals, without which no great kind of species can be organised in its existence or in its desired perfection. For example, God knew well in eternity that people, if created in such-and-such composition, and their administration is given such-and-such celestial shape, then mischief will spread among them unavoidably, and they would follow the improper course in many of their affairs. It then became necessary in the wisdom of God to send a Sagacious man among them, the raising of whose power and rank, and the preservation of whose religion for a long time has been already decided by God. He knew well that such-and-such a one is more fitted to be that Sagacious man. Such a one was a person who, when he appeared in the beginning, appeared like the species. Thus he became a Singular man as good as the species itself.

Similarly, God knew that when people are gathered on the Judgment Day, many of them will be found condemned by their corrupt deeds and that a remedy for this lay with the "Great grace" (namely the Sagacious man, the Prophet), who will cleanse their hearts and purify them. However, the consideration of all these points and the appearance of the mercy of God were not possible save through the agency of the Sagacious person, exclusively devoted to God for the intercession of His creation, the one who should have so trained himself in the service of the Divine light as to have become His instrument in the creation and His interpreter among the people.

God knew this all in eternity, and when the form of the Sagacious person appeared, it appeared like the species. Similarly, the affairs (of people) would not be set in proper order except through the appearance of the souls breathed into luminous bodies (angels of the Sublime Assembly). God knew them in eternity, and when their forms appeared, they appeared like the species. Among them are Gabriel, Mika'il, Israfil, Izra'il, the chiefs of the Sublime Assembly and the bearers of the Throne, who are always praying for mankind.

Lamha 41

Similarly, the name of angel is applied to the faculties and the capabilities of the Great Body. Their origin is the emanation of the universe in the way that the "Essential grace" requires. Many a time these faculties put on the dress of particularisation and representation in the

Similitudinary World. And then because of that, they are
called angels. In this connection, there is a Tradition that
not a drop of rain ever comes down but an angel accompanies it who never ascends again. It is also narrated that
in sleep, such-and-such a dream appeared to a man in
such-and-such form.

Lamha 42

The largest class of angels is that of the patterns of
species. Their influence in this connection is great. The
reason is that when the Universal Soul through contemplation understands the systems of species in detail and
the qualities they possess, and the souls of the celestial
spheres and others also come in line with that understanding by coincidence, then the patterns of the species
in their Similitudinary forms happen to stand before their
Lord pleading for His grace for their appearance in the
world of mortals, and for the complete and perfect
appearance of their predications as far as it may be
possible. Sometimes, when the heavenly and the earthly
causes unite for their appearance, the Patterns are given
what they have been pleading for. But if a certain thing
obstructs their appearance, and hinders them from
achieving their desired object, it is rejected and dis-
approved of because of their extremely pressing requirement for it.

At times the causes unite for giving a punishment
which is to completely destroy the species as a whole, but
there the Patterns plead in the language expressed by
their condition and not in the language of their tongue
for the preservation of their images on the earth. It is the
reason why the prophet Noah was ordered to carry in
the boat a pair from every species, male and female.
The Holy Prophet had once ordered the killing of dogs,
but then he disliked that, and said "they are also one of
the communities". This was so because the Patterns
stood before their Lord pleading for the existence of the
form of their image on the earth.

Similarly, the name of angel is applied to the human souls joined to the first two species of the angels. They hover round the Throne and are completely attracted towards it. No hindrance hinders them from it. They become a cause for the descent of the grace of God, the ears for hearing the prayers of the people of earth, and the tongues for many a suitable inspiration. On that account, the more the things of this kind increase by the increase of the (praying) persons in the latter half of the night the more often the contention takes place among them (the angels). God has said "I (Muhammad) have no knowledge of the Sublime Assembly when they contend among themselves".[1] Their contention, however, is not by way of a quarrel, or a debate, or a challenge or an opposition. But God has two providences according to every particular order. And for every order, there is an external providence of the Sublime Assembly. It (Sublime Assembly) is entrusted with it, is urged toward it and is commanded to pray for it. Sometimes, when two intentions oppose one another, without any idea of opposition, then God gives a decisive judgment according to the Universal Expediency represented before Him.

Lamha 43

Similarly, the name of angel is applied to the souls puffed into fine bodies dominated by air at the time of the happy conjunctions of the stars, particularly when there is a handsome commingling of the planets Jupiter, Saturn and the Moon. These angels are of different categories. There are some which become an army of the planets Saturn, Jupiter and Mars, etc. Some of them, according to their different conditions, become a shadow of the Sublime Assembly, and serve as an army of Gabriel and Mika'il. Some among them, because of their natural disposition, are the servants of the Divine Names, and the Qur'anic verses. At times some people,

---

[1] Surah, Sad, V. 69.

through the use of what sets the powers of the stars in motion, compel the armies of the stars. And they, by their invocation of God, compel the armies of the Sublime Assembly. Their invocation renders the human mind like them. They also compel the armies of the Servants, a class of angels, through their continuous recitation of the fixed words.

Lamha 44

I have seen many a wonder in the case of these angels. There came an extremely auspicious form requiring penetration into the fine constitution which led towards the puffing of a soul. All the fine elements which were there on that day between the heaven and the earth mixed up together and formed a fine mixture. From that mixture a putrefaction was produced, just as is found in the mixture of elements when the soul is puffed into the bodies of the insects of earth, such as the frog and the gnat, etc. When the fine elements putrefied, a suitable soul was puffed into them. The conditions of these angels, however, differ on account of the celestial forms and the four elements. They have, therefore, no power of nutrition and of growth in them. But the souls have two aspects, one towards the preservation of the body alone and the other towards the High origins.

Some are like a fine body, round and hexagonal, etc., like a house on earth of different shapes and sizes. When a spiritual predication suitable to those souls descends from above, either from the side of the stars or the Sublime Assembly or from the movement of the Similitudinary bodies or from the souls which are represented in the Similitudinary World, the incentives arise in their hearts, just as they arise in the insects of earth on account of their natures. And just as, when some insects see the light, they turn towards it, because of an incentive which arises from the very root of their nature, similarly, when they (insects) feel heat, they run away from the hot earth to the cold, and from the dampness towards the dryness.

In the same manner, when the incentive arises from their hearts like a natural course, then the great armies of angels gather where God desires. Each one of them carries love or hatred for a thing with the result that the aspect of that incentive (of love or hatred) gets imprinted upon the minds of men and animals present there, and then they start working accordingly.

Lamha 45

Similarly, the name of angel is applied to the similitudinary forms of words and deeds which proceed from man. Its reality is that among other souls the condition of the human souls is rather important and wonderful. It is so because they have been created from a source very near to the Holy Fold. The angels around it (Holy Fold) which bear the Throne and those which manage the affairs (of the universe) are attracted towards them with a natural attraction, and are moved towards them with the result that they settle down in them (souls) for a long time.

There are words and deeds which, when a man utters and practises them continuously for a long time, assume a certain form both in the Holy Fold and in the perceptive faculties of the great angels. The celestial spheres then accept that form. Thus the perceptive faculties of the celestial spheres become a matter for the faculties of the angels. Their (celestial spheres') cognitions harmonize, and then turn into forms standing before the Real (God), neither to be attributed to a particular celestial sphere nor to any angel in particular. At that time, those forms are named "angels". The reason is that they have similitudinary bodies and stable forms, and possess souls which are the meanings understood from those words. They are a ready vision before the great angels and the souls.

Indeed, these forms of words and deeds resemble the angels in the similitudinary substances. Therefore when a reciter recites those words and a doer does those deeds, a wide road opens up from the root of his mind towards their similitudinary reality. There the mind receives suitable blessings and becomes like this kind of angel. They exercise a great influence upon the human mind with respect to the laws which are decided there.

Lamha 46

Similarly, the name of angel is applied to a community of people. They receive such inspiration that their minds become perplexed in accepting and going by it. Just as an aspect works with the natural incentive of hunger, thirst and lust, etc., gets completely lost in it (incentive) and prevails over its five senses until both its outward and inward are filled with that (aspect), and if at that time there had been some clear-minded person whose self had been struck by it, he would have seen his outward and inward self dyed with the dye of that incentive; similarly, a Divine or angelic thought springs up in the mind of "this person", prevails upon it, gets lost in it, dominates its five senses to such an extent that the person looks as if he is perplexed, bewildered or even mad, until God executes the order which was to be carried out. So long as he is under that aspect, he is called an "angel".

Sometimes an animal accepts the inspiration and works for it. At that time it is said that an angel has appeared in the form of an animal.

Lamha 47

The form of Administration is that all the causes, the requirements and (Divine) Providence according to every cause should be taken into consideration. It happens in this way that all those things which the relative good near to the absolute good requires on that day, are made available in abundance, as far as it may be possible. If there are causes requiring evil and they cannot appear without a cause of "good", and barring the elements, they may originate in the imagination and the fancy of the Sublime Assembly; then it becomes necessary that it (cause of good) may be included in the suitable flow of the universal order, so that there should be no disruption in the predication of the celestial spirituality and the natures of these elements. The reason is that created science is weaker and meaner than the Divine science, and also because the Administration is an attribute, which is tested against the Creation. As such, it is proper that no predication should be broken. If the Administration bears a weak connection with spirituality, and some good for the "born one" is desired, then that (good) is poured over the earth, which, however, does not become completely effective except after some time when it happens to become a power of spirituality. Consequently, the human existence will be composed of that power, and the whole affair will become complete. But if there is earthly connection which necessitates the death of a beloved, while according to the celestial powers the time of his separation from the world had not come as yet, then his death would be found in some other cause, conflicting however with the normal course. The predication of the earthly connection (demanding his death) would be resisted, and the beloved will live as before. Such an example is found in the fire of Abraham. An extremely cold and blessed wind blew over the fire, prevailed upon it and changed it into coolness and safety.

If the causes were to so require, it will fit in many ways. One is "the expanded way" and the other is "the contracted way". The best order will give its decision on that. The fire for example, at times, proves effective by burning, and turns the burnt thing into ashes. Or it effects in this way that the burning object may feel pain, but may not perish. In this case, however, it is not blessed, with the result that it is extinguished. Nay, it is also the decision that the Divine Providence may be taken into consideration according to every cause. When the stars' conjunctions demand the death of a person, and the calamity to overtake him is also decided, then the right course according to his bodily constitution would be that there should be a cause of death in his body, however weak it may be. If a physician were to examine such cases for a thousand years, he will not understand them as against the bodily constitution, but only through expansion and contraction. When the conjunctions of the stars require the life of a man, who was otherwise to die according to his bodily constitution, but whose safety had also been decided, then in that case the presence of a bodily cause is necessary to maintain the natural power of the body or an antidote is made available to save his life. If a mathematician were to test such a case a thousand times, he will not understand it as against the heavenly order but only by means of contraction and expansion.

There is a man who is engrossed in bestial pleasures. When God desires to give him guidance, and if there is no hindrance in the way, such as the hardness of his heart and his obedience to the devil, then He will inspire in his heart a clear inspiration or does so through reminding him of the requirements of his nature, with the result that it (inspiration) will necessarily invite him to the straight path. If there are two aspects in him, namely an aspect of obedience and an aspect of disobedience, then only through the aspect of obedience can the inspiration shine. He (inspired one) in this case will remain in hesitation till the Divine help appears to him clearly.

Many a man falls in destruction and is encompassed by it. He begins to supplicate God or may not supplicate, but the heavenly causes have not decided for his death as yet. Then God inspires his heart with a device of deliverance from that destruction or inspires him with some thing which prepares a way for his deliverance, etc., till all those things combined together will lead to his deliverance. Or some natural order is weakened with the result that the deliverance is achieved. This natural order otherwise would break the universal order, but was itself broken by God.

Some people are taken unawares while they are

negligent. They are then guided aright to self-preservation by means of a dream or an inspiration or through a warning of a prophet or a reformer. For example, once when a believer had looked at the cloud, he had come to know through the revelation of his acoustic sense that it (cloud) is asking him to water the garden of so-and-so. This is told in a Tradition.

There is a person in whom, when God sees the penetration of the auspicious powers of the celestial spheres, He inspires the hearts of people who are to deal with him, such as his companions, his women-folk and his servants to do that in which lies his good and his happiness. Or he himself is blessed in his views with the result that he is guided to a fine and pleasant life, or comes near to the good. For example, if he goes to one of his friends, all of a sudden he meets someone who does good to him, or if he walks over a slippery place it causes weakness in his foot, with the result that, he falls on the ground and lo! there he finds a treasure. The people on such an occasion say that he is lucky and fortunate.

There is many a man in whom, when God sees the penetration of the harmful powers of the celestial spheres, He inspires the hearts of people with hatred for him, with the result that he does not succeed in his aim. Though he sees dreams, they do not fit in with his aim. Sometimes, when he goes to one of his friends, his enemy all of a sudden comes across him, and in consequence, he is grieved. Or at times he is inspired with anger for one walking with him, who in turn strikes and abuses him. Thus, he finds the evil result of his blow and abuse extremely painful. Or he walks over a slippery place with the result that his foot breaks. The people at that time say that he is wretched and unlucky.

What is necessary to know here is that when God desires to do something and the Divine wisdom requires it to be done quickly, but earthly causes are not favourable, then no hindrance hinders Him from completing His object, whatever the cause may be. The reason is that God possesses infinite knowledge of every event, so that if He were to suppress this and expand that, it would be this, and if He were to suppress that and expand this, it would be that, and so on *ad infinitum.*

Lamha 48

Verily God is Living, is Self-subsistent, is the Knower of all universals and particulars. The knowledge of some other thing in this respect in no way conflicts with Him. He is the Seeing, the Hearing and the Powerful over all possibilities. The willer of what He decides, and is the active doer of what He desires. He speaks through inspiration in the hearts of His servants, by calling them from behind the veil, and by means of sending an angel, who appears before them in a certain form and reveals with His permission what He likes. He superintends every soul as to what it is doing, takes account of people's actions and brings them (actions) back to them. He then rewards the obedient and punishes the disobedient. He gets both pleased and angry, raises and lowers, responds to the call of the constrained (and dispels the distress of the distressed). He is the Director, the Wise, the Just, doing nothing but what is truth and wherein lies the Universal Expediency for the thing. He knows all in detail, but our knowledge falls short.

Before going too deeply into explaining these words, you should know that the reality of these attributes of God cannot be taken in the sense of the existence of their preliminaries which are "passivities" and "renewals" as God transcends all this, but rather in the sense of the existence of their ends. All the ends are included in the Administration in consideration of the "best order", and in view of the Divine grace which descends according to every condition and time, even though there are renewals in these attributes. All this has recourse to the eternal attribute which does not admit of any renewal or change in itself. It is the guardian of the Divine grace and truth. Its renewal is taken only in the sense of its appearance in many forms and wonderful emanations according to the condition of the world accepting its grace. By this point is meant that the attributes of God are eternal and their relations are temporal. These attributes are proved for God in consideration of His being the maintainer of the Universal nature, to the point that it penetrates the whole of the world of mortals, its limbs and its faculties, and not in consideration of His Essence.

There are three things before you, namely a living one, a dead one and a lifeless one. The living, however, is the nearest one in bearing resemblance to what is there (God). And because, He is the knower and effective in creation, it became necessary to name Him as the Living one. Since knowledge in our opinion means disclosure, and all the things which were included in His person and those which are present are disclosed to Him in detail, it became necessary that He be named as the Knower.

As seeing and hearing are a complete disclosure of both the audible and the visible, similarly they are there (in God) in the utmost perfect form. Thus, it became necessary that He be named as the Hearing and the Seeing.

When we say "He willed" it only means the goodness of His decision for doing an act or abandoning it. God is doing many of His works when the required condition is present, or when the world becomes ready for them. At that time He necessitates the creation of a thing which otherwise it was not necessary to create. At times, a consensus of opinion is arrived at by His permission and wisdom in some higher planes when it was not there before. It then became necessary that He should be named as the Willer.

By the essential, eternal and singular will is also meant the requirement of the Essence when it once became related to the whole world. Then happenings followed day after day, and it became correct to attribute the will to every happening separately. Thus it is said "He willed this and this".

When we say that such a one has power, we only mean thereby that he has become able to do a thing, and no external cause can prevent him from doing that. As regards the preference which the powerful gives to the powerless, it in no way rejects the name of power. God has power over everything, and by His kindness and His Essential requirement gives preference to some works over others. It therefore became necessary to name Him the Powerful.

When we say that such a one spoke to such a one, by that we only mean the transmission of intended ideas linked up with words indicative of them (those ideas). God often times pours knowledge over His servant and pours with it the required words indicative of (knowledge) which get settled in his mind, so that it should be the most necessary thing for teaching. Thus, it became necessary to call Him the Speaking one. God says: "It is not fitting for a man that God should speak to him except by revelation or from behind a veil, or He may send a messenger, who may reveal to him with His permission what He likes; verily He has power over everything".[1]

Revelation means the breathing into the heart through a dream or by creating the necessary knowledge in it at the time when man concentrates upon the Unseen. Or he may hear a well-arranged speech from behind the veil, as if he hears it from outside but does not see its speaker. Or God may send a messenger, then an angel may appear to him in a certain form. Often times, during his concentration upon the Unseen when the senses are suppressed, he hears a voice like that of the chime of a bell, just as a man in a state of swoon (caused, for example, by a severe blow on the head) sees various colours such as red and black.

There is an order in the Holy Fold, and the people are required to establish it. If they fit themselves for this, they will join the Sublime Assembly, will be brought out from darkness to the light of God and to His bliss and will be made happy. Both the angels and men will be

[1] Qu'ran, Surah Shura, V. 51.

inspired to do good to them. But if they do not fit themselves for that order, they will be cursed by the Sublime Assembly, incur its anger and will be punished as mentioned before. Thus, it became necessary to say: God became pleased, thankful or angry and is cursing. All this returns to the course the world follows according to the requirement of the Universal Expediency.

Often times, the order of the world requires that a thing for which prayer is made may be created, and then it is said: God accepted the prayer.

Sometimes we use the word "seeing" in the sense of the most complete possible disclosure of the seen thing. When people after death will be moved to what they were promised in the future life, they will join the Manifestation which stands in the middle of the Similitudinary World, and will see everything clearly with their own eyes. It, therefore, became necessary to say: "Verily you will soon see your Lord, just as you see the moon on the night of the full moon".[1]

Lamha 49

This manifestation (one standing in the middle of the Similitudinary World) is of many turns and modes according to its appearance with the past predications at different times. Such a reference is made in the Word of God: "Every day He is in new splendour".[2] We shall explain here the difference of both the beginning and the end of this age we are in, so that it may become a model for knowing the difference.

Let it be remembered that the happenings in the beginning of this age were the result of the powers of the celestial spheres and elements, and of nothing else. Once a thought occurred to the mind of Enoch (*Idries, Idris, Edris, Idriss,* etc.) to know the movements of the stars and their properties and also to know the events before their

---

[1] Reference to the Tradition.
[2] Qu'ran, Surah Rahman, V. 29.

happening from the point of view of those movements and properties. Some time passed in this way. Then the strength of the Sublime Assembly increased. It increased only because such conjunctions of the heavenly bodies had taken place as necessitated the flow of the Universal Soul in the physical forms made of the vapour of elements. This is how the human souls were produced, characterised by qualities which were suitable to the world of the celestial souls. When he (Enoch) died, many causes similar to what we have mentioned joined the Sublime Assembly.

When the strength of the Sublime Assembly increased and its knowledge and concentration combined, the Divine wisdom made it necessary that its (Sublime Assembly's) concentration should represent the predications of the Great Body, and should in some way make preparation for its necessary requirements. From that day, the predications of astronomy became null and void. I mean thereby that its clear predication about everything became obsolete. Thus knowledge of important matters and of general utility measures in advance cannot be had. The astronomer cannot find any figures about them nor can he even think of them.

In the case of a thing about which the celestial powers differ as to whether it may happen or not, and there is a likelihood that it may not happen, but the likelihood of its happening may be strong, the astronomer cannot give any decision. It is so because the suppression and the expansion of the causes is the business of the Sublime Assembly. When a man concentrates upon it, he comes to know of the Execution which is to descend. Hence there is no need of knowing the rules of the stars and their movements.

Thereafter, new sciences sprang up in the heart of Abraham, in the light of which he digressed from the stars and devoted himself to the Sublime Assembly with the result that the column of the concentration of the Sublime Assembly, and the column of the reward based on deeds became strong. The column of the celestial

62

powers regarding happenings and events became correspondingly weak, and the commandment of the Laws ruled absolute. The angelic suppression came very near to man and the Great Emanation appeared in the form of the creed. The devotion to God was linked with prayer, purity, belief in the angels, the Scriptures, the prophets and in the absorption in the light of God.

When the Holy Prophet came and the Great Emanation also descended towards the Similitudinary World, the whole thing became complete. Surely he (Holy Prophet) came to perfect noble qualities.

Lamha 50

Verily this (Great) Emanation sheds lights and reflections which appear like the reflections of the sun, and like the reflections of the other luminous bodies in mirrors of different kinds and dimensions. These reflections and these lights are also termed the Emanation and the Descent. Sometimes, on account of the permanency of the Emanations or because of their establishment in the external world, the true predications are attributed to God.

Often times when one sees such a light or reflection in his dream, it is said "So-and-so saw his Lord in his dream or in his wakefulness".

At times God speaks to us by means of an Emanation, and then it is said "So-and-so spoke with his Lord".

Sometimes the knowledge of future events before their actual happening appears in a certain plane according to the Emanation, and then on that occasion it is said "God appeared in such-and-such a way".

At times, in a plane where those lights are crossing each other and those emanations are opposing one another, an aspect of joy and happiness is produced, which appears in the Similitudinary World like the gleam of dawn in the horizon. At that time it is said "God has smiled, laughed, is pleased and delighted".

Sometimes a contrary aspect is produced, which

represents His retribution and His hatred in the Similitudinary World. At that time it is said "God has cursed,
is displeased, has become angry and sorry for".

The Law has not used these words carelessly but because it did not find in the language the people know and
are familiar with any other words clearer than these.

Lamha 51

Know that the emanations, however numerous they
may be, their origin is the three principles, and they are
as follows:—

(1) The intellectual form of knowledge, which is
imprinted upon the perceptive faculties, is an image of
that knowledge. That is so because the intellectual form
has two aspects. In one aspect, it is an accident, existing
by the knower itself, but in this aspect it is not correctly
applicable to the known. In another aspect, however, it
unites with knowledge in some way. In this aspect, it
(form) is the emanation of knowledge in the perceptive
process. On the basis of this principle it is said "I have
seen such a one in a dream" and "I have seen the moon
in a cup of water".

When a gnostic (Arif, the realised Sufi, 'he who has
esoteric knowledge') concentrates upon the form of his
belief in his Lord, a form corresponding to his belief is
represented, and then that form becomes an instrument
of revealing his Lord, and an instrument to introduce the
gnostic to his self. As long as this concentration, belief and
the introduction are there, they will continue to be the
image of the Necessary Being and His emanation.

(2) The concentration of the strong spirit of an angel
or of a superior person, adheres to some portion of an
elemental matter or a similitudinary faculty. And this
concentration is like matter for the similitudinary
existing things. If that concentration adheres in such a
way as to become an introduction to God and His form,
then that form would be His emanation. If for example it
adheres in such a way that it becomes a cause for bring-

ing unity among the people, a case which may take place by the order of the Divine Administration, then that form, if it appears as an event, would be a blessing. Or if it happens to be a substance, then it will be one of the signs of God, such as the Ka'ba, the Qur'an, the prayer and the Law. Sometimes, when the concentrations of the angels are focussed upon a particular place, there appears some kind of blessing, and in that blessing shines the Divine light.

(3) There is some hidden point in every being proceeding from the Divine Essence. It is in this way that Zaid, for example, if looked into very deeply, will be found to be man, animal, body, speaker, feeler, willer, grower, walker, writer, laugher, poet, Roman, Negro, and so on. Each one of these predications truly fits in with him. These predications are true not because a considerer has made such a consideration and a supposer has made such a supposition, but because there is an origin of this predication in the external world, by which all these were proved to be true. And also because there was no origin of any other predication, by which they were proved to be false. Each one of them (man, animal, body, etc.) whether it is from essentials or from accidentals, is a general reality, represented in relation to this individual and fitting in with it. Thus, opposite each one of them there is a point in one of the planes in reality. The point which arises from our saying "It exists by the Being Whose existence is self-necessitated, flows from Him, and is an emanation of His bounty" is that shining point which refers to the Divine Essence, and is an imitation and an image of it.

All individuals and beings are not equal (of the same level of purity), but there are individuals who are dominated by the predications of the low, inferior points. Some are dominated by the predications of the superior points which correspond to the Universal Administration, the Universal Expediency and to the aspect of abstraction. The plane of God facing this point is the Divine Emanation which shines in the heart of every gnostic, and in the heart of every creature. When all these three principles unite and meet at one place in the heart of man, then the reflection of the Emanation and of the Divine light will be complete and perfect. But if there is only one principle (and the other two are wanting), then one reality of the Emanation will be reflected in it. Contemplate this, as it is a difficult problem.

Lamha 52

A Great Emanation will appear for people on the Day of Resurrection. They will see it as they used to see the sun and the moon in the world. The reality of it is that the light which we have already mentioned will appear in a form the (origin of) humanity will require. The reason is that humanity is a model and a balance for all that is poured upon the individuals of the human species, and you will not find any individual going outside that balance. The belief of human individuals in their Lord and the knowledge they have about Him have a limit for each one of them which they cannot cross.

On the Day of Resurrection God will manifest Himself in the form of that limit. It will be a universal and general emanation of which, when it appears to them, they will have no doubt. They, however, will differ in the identification of that very emanation. Thus everyone will see it in a form corresponding to his particular belief. This is the meaning of what has come down in the Tradition that God will appear to the unbelievers in a form which the believers will not like.

The universal, general emanation is present in the external (world), and is held great in the Similitudinary World. Its origin is the Great Body and the general belief of man. As far as the particular emanations are concerned, they will see them with their own eyes, as when a man keeps a red glass before his eye, and sees everything as red, or keeps a green one, and sees everything as green, while the thing seen is one and the same in both the cases.

Lamha 53

There is one emanation which comes down to the terrestrial heaven every night when there remains only the last one third of it. Its reality is that there is one secret of the Unseen concealed in the Sun and the planet Venus. The strongest effect of this secret is found on earth at a time when both these happen to be in the "four quarters".[1] The Holy Prophet has made everything clear and has mentioned its property.

The property of the quarter which is above the earth is that the actions are presented before God, and by that is meant that they are accepted by Him. The reason being that at that time the rays radiating from their actions shine with utmost brilliancy. There are natures in the other quarter, and what is understood from it is that the angels spread on the earth, come by turns, and carry the actions of people to God. It is so because the angels bear relation to the planet Venus, and the prayer has relation to the Sun.

The angels spread in the quarter which is under the earth with the result that the Divine light shines in it (earth). At that time it is said "Verily, God comes down to the terrestrial heaven and says 'Is there anyone to ask for forgiveness?' ".[2]

The time of the stay of the Sun in the quarters has not been specified. It, however, has become a case moving between the state which was found a little before the stay and the state which was found a little after the stay. It is so because Venus sometimes is preceded by the Sun and at times is succeeded by it. They are like sailors in a boat. The boat may help them (Sun and Venus) in their properties or may not help them but it never goes wrong for a long period.

Investigation has shown that the centre of moment is

---

[1] This probably refers to the four fixed signs of the Zodiac: Taurus, Leo, Scorpio and Aquarius.

[2] This is a reference to the Tradition.

very small. On that account the Holy Prophet has said "In the days of your age your Lord has gusts of favour; then place yourself in the way of them".

Lamha 54

There is an emanation which is spread in the souls of the angels and in those of superior men. The truth about it is that the extremely sublime souls are turned towards this emanation according to their capabilities. Their case is just like the case of the mirrors of different dimensions and colours placed around a lamp. Thus a thing suitable to the mirror will be reflected in it, and all the spreading rays will collect in it. Or their case is like the case of the sun rising over watering-troughs and pools of different sizes and colours in which its form is reflected.

If some form takes place in the earth which is liked by the Sublime Assembly, then it will survive in the Real and will be lost in It. Just as the colours of the rays of the souls come down from this emanation, similarly some aspects can be conceived of them (souls), which prove effective in those rays to a certain extent. The reason being that they (aspects) appear according to the (purity of the) souls. The aspects in the rays, however, have connection with the souls. Thus an assumed aspect appears interpreted as cheerfulness. Similarly an aspect of anger goes up, named displeasure, anger and grief.

Sometimes a form of an event which is to take place in the near future appears in these rays. At that time it is said "A new thing has appeared for God". This situation puts the prophets to a hard test. Here are the words of God: "Or have you thought that you would be left free while Allah does not yet know those of you who will fight for Him and does not know the patient?"[1]

This verse with other verses plainly speaks of the renewal of their (sublime persons') knowledge. It has been proved to us that this renewed knowledge is proved

[1] Qur'an, Surah Taubah, V. 16.

for God by means of this emanation. When the souls of believers are dyed with the colours of purity, those with that aspect ascend endlessly towards the Sublime Assembly. In consequence the aspect of this emanation also ascends. Nothing can make this meaning more clear than the saying "God knew that they will fight, so He liked them".

Lamha 55

There is one emanation which the Holy Prophet saw in his sleep in a most beautiful form. "It had placed its hand on his shoulder." An elucidation of the secret of this emanation is that the man who has known God, inevitably believes that He possesses the perfect attributes, free from any form and colour. Every attribute, however, has a particular form and colour. For example, bravery, if it is to appear in a dream, would appear in the form of a lion, in the shape of a young man dressed in a coat of mail, with a sword in his hand and so on.

Sometimes the image of the attributes of God appears to man in his commonsense in certain forms and colours. Now when the form is the revealer of those attributes, and is the instrument of knowing them, then it is one of the emanations of God. In a case like this, it is correct to say that he saw God.

Lamha 56

There is one emanation which the prophet Moses saw at the mountain Tur in the form of fire. An elucidation of this secret is that he deserved to be sent by God to Pharaoh to teach him what He wills, true knowledge to the extent that it may not require any further clarification. With Moses the material knowledge was the superior one. As such, the Divine wisdom required that he be addressed with a voice in which there should be no doubt of its being from God, and that that voice should be a perceptible one. Accordingly, He inspired in the minds (*Qulub*, also lit. 'hearts') of some angels of the Sublime Assembly to turn towards this tree and assume there the form of the light and image of God. They then assumed a strong form with the result that their assumption opened one of the doors of the Similitudinary World. Consequently the element of air of that place took the colour of the form of fire, which revealed the address of God, as the form reflected in the mirror reveals one who looks in it. In a case like this, the concentration of the Sublime Assembly is necessary so that the elements in that place assume the required colours.

Lamha 57

There is one emanation about which the Christians believe that it is the Divinity which has put on the dress of humanity, and the Hindus take it as an incarnation of God in the perfect man. God removed this confusion by saying in the Holy Qur'an "And We strengthened him (Christ) through the Holy Spirit".[1] From this it became clear that in reality it was the strength of the Holy Spirit which liars took to be the appearance of the Deity in the form of man and an incarnation. "God is far above what the unjust say."[2]

The reality of that emanation is that the Universal Soul does not descend as a particular one, but in the form the world requires on that day. If it descends on a day when the Sun happens to be in its own house, then it will be the Sun in its house in the particular soul. And if it descends when the Sun happens to be in the east, then it will be the Sun in the east in the particular soul. Similarly if it descends when the Sun is in its own like (*Mathal*, 'equivalence'), then it will be the Sun in its own like in the particular soul. These are the degrees of the power of the Sun, and the stages of the appearance of its effect upon the soul.

[1] Qur'an, Surah Baqarah, V. 253.
[2] Qur'an, Surah Bani Israil, V. 43.

On this analogy it is proper to know that when the Universal Soul descends as a particular one, then the form of the Great Emanation will appear in it. And why not? As the Great Emanation is the heart of the Universal Soul and the mainstay of its affairs. As such it is more entitled than the Sun and the Moon to appear in it. The point opposite to the Great Emanation in the particular soul is named the "Pure Intellect".

People, however, differ in the "Pure Intellect" on account of the difference of the degrees in the appearance of the Great Emanation, like the difference we find in the degrees of the Sun. Thus the "Pure Intellect" in some people will be found shining brilliantly. There is an open, wide road between it and the Great Emanation. Therefore there is always a standing shadow of the Great Emanation on the "Pure Intellect". Consequently the rays of the "Pure Intellect" fall on the soul, the secret (*Sirr*, also 'innermost consciousness') and the other faculties (*Lata'if*, also 'organs of higher perception') between them. The man then becomes Divine from one aspect and a human from the other aspect, and turns out to be an extraordinary person. You will see extraordinary signs in him, particularly in perfecting defective minds, in causing Divine blessings to flow and in the redeeming of their sins.

Many a time an emanation from the Great Emanation appearing in the creation takes place, but happens to be rather less bright. However, at times there seems to be no difference between the two, particularly when people have the powerful illusion that Divinity has put on the dress of a human being or that God has entered into some (perfect) mind. God, therefore, removed this confusion and said that it is only the strength of the Holy Spirit in the minds. By the Holy Spirit is meant "This Great Emanation", and by his (person's) being strengthened means that he comes under its blessings, and in those blessings its shadow takes a certain form so that it looks like the Great Emanation itself.

Lamha 58

There is one emanation to which God has made reference in the Holy Qur'an. "He rules the affair from heaven to earth, then in the end it (affair) ascends towards Him on a day the space whereof will be equal to one thousand years according to your reckoning."[1] Again His words are "Every day He is in new splendour".[2] The reason is that when the conditions of heaven and earth come up to a stage which makes it necessary in the Universal Expediency for the Great Emanation to assume a colour other than its first one, then it will have a Universal splendour. This is how the Great Emanation descends. It, however, will be according to the image of man in the Similitudinary World. A thing's being the image of a thing on the basis of truth has made some accidents and substances to have a natural relation with some created things. Just as when you think of Zaid as red and tall and 'Amr as black and short, then you have two different forms in your mind. This is not because of their colours and sizes, but because of some natural relation which some have with the others, so that every created thing may be distinguished by its natural distinguishing marks.

Similarly, in the Similitudinary World some are distinguished from other created things, contrary to the Great Emanation. At the time of certain celestial conjunctions (of the stars), the Great Emanation descends towards the earth. The angels continue to work in support of the predication of its descent, and neglect those the neglect of which is made necessary by its descent. The reason being that the obedient is he who obeys the predication of God according to the descent, and the disobedient is he who disobeys Him according to this descent, till the form of the Great Emanation changes and it (Great Emanation) takes some other form. When

---

[1] Qur'an, Surah Sajda, V. 5.
[2] Qur'an, Surah Rahman, V. 29.

it takes some other form, this last descent ascends upwards and its predications are disseminated. The meaning of the words of God "He rules the affair from the
heaven to the earth" is that He rules the world and its
working order so that that affair, after having been made
as a similitudinary body, descends towards the earth, the
angels are made to serve it, and the world is prepared for
that (affair). When the appointed time comes to an end,
that affair ascends towards God and then some other
affair similar to it descends. Thus this process of descent
and ascent continues for a long time. When one descent
comes to an end, the ascent starts. The extent of that
duration is generally one thousand years approximately.
The great prophets are raised only after the end of this
duration (namely one thousand years). The reason is that
God knows the Law suitable to the age. He therefore
appoints for men one who may compel them to follow
that Law, and be the interpreter of that age (*Qarn*, also
'centuries'). The persons other than the prophets are
raised only as the renovators (*Mujaddidun*, 'renewers') of
the earlier Law, a mercy for people to perfect their
qualities.

Lamha 59

Now when you have known these four perfections,
you should also know that, while defining the realities,
the course followed by the prophets is to keep silent on
points like Divinity, Intellect, Soul and Matter. The first
thing they tell their people is that the intelligible
(*Mafhum*, 'that which is understood, perceived') is confined to two words, namely the existent and the non-
existent. By existent they mean that which exists both in
the external world and in the realities. In other words,
what is established (*Muhaqqiq*, also 'verified') both in the
Soul and in Matter. This is a thing which is interpreted
as "Bil-Kharij". By non-existent they mean that which
neither exists in the external world nor in the stage of
latency before existence.

The existent is either necessary and eternal or possible (*Mumkin*) and temporal (*Hadith*). The Necessary Who exists externally is one Who exists by His Essence (Whose existence is identical with Its Essence). By it (Necessary) they mean, that Emanation (*Tajalli*, 'shining forth') which is caused by the external in its very beginning. The Emanation is an abstract reality, and transcends all that is close to the sublime aspects of the Soul. By possible they mean that which is close to its (Soul's) low aspects. It (possible) is subject to change and involves both creation and destruction (*Kawn wa fisad*). Every possible is temporal and happens by the will of God. The giving of order in relation to the happenings is, however, different from the Will. To advance a proof of this is not the business of the prophets. Praise be to God in the beginning, in the end, outwardly and inwardly.

SATA'AT

All praise be to God, the giver of bounties and the inspirer of wisdom. Blessings and benedictions be on His messenger, the noblest, who was given the Qur'an (in which many meanings are comprised in a few words) and on his family and Companions, the best of his community, which again is the best of all communities. I bear witness that there is no god but God alone Who has no partner, and that Muhammad is His servant and His messenger. May God send His blessings and benedictions upon him, his family and his Companions.

Now after this the needy (*Faqir*) Waliyullah says that these are a few words entitled "Sata'at" (Illuminations), an explanation of the Divine Secret which is a link between the Abstract pure and the Visible world and some of its properties and consequences. I beseech God for help and on Him I rely.[1]

Sat' 1

To begin with: Being in the sense of Reality and not as a concept is of three stages, and they are as follows:

(1) Pure Essence.
(2) Stage of Intellect.
(3) Stage of the Great Body (*Shakhs akbar*).

The emanation of the stage of Intellect from Pure Essence is by way of necessity and the requirement of the Essence itself, just as the number four requires the presence of "even" in our intellectual faculty, and is like

[1] By the Divine Secret is meant the Divine Manifestation (*Tajalli*).

the spread of light from the disc of the sun in the world outside[1].

Shakhs Akbar is also emanated from the Pure Essence just as the Intellect is emanated from it. An example of this emanation is as though we engraved the word "Zaid" on a ring, but had not as yet struck the ring on wax or clay. The existence of the image of "Zaid", however, though in general it lasts as long as the ring lasts, is acquired in one respect, namely that it is "Zaid" and not "Amr", and not acquired in another respect, namely that if it is engraved on wax it would be one thing and if engraved on clay it would be another. We then bring wax or clay and strike the ring on it with the result that a particular engraving appears, penetrating the wax or clay at that time. The first is universal and the second is particular; one is intellect and the other is visibility.

This actual penetrating engraving has two aspects. In one aspect it is contained in the ring itself and in the other in the wax or in the clay. When both these aspects are actually combined together at one place, Shakhs Akbar really comes into existence, and by that one existence, both the aspects actually come into existence. Think over this deeply.

Sat' 2

Shakhs Akbar by its being one of the unities is one thing; but when we split it, two parts become manifest. The Universal Soul and the Rahmani Soul. The Universal Soul is a penetrating one and a determiner while the Rahmani Soul is an object of penetration (*Mahal*) and a substratum (*Mudu'a*).

When we cause water to boil until the whole of it is turned into steam, its watery form disappears and instead the airy form appears. The alternate succession of both is on one and the same vehicle, which is their matter (*Hyula*). This matter, however, has no name, nor

---

[1] By Pure Essence is meant God, Who is also sometimes called "Ghaib-ul-Ghaib".

is it necessary for it to have any name. This water has a name and that is "water" and this air has also a name and that is "steam". The effect of water wherever it be is coolness, freshness and pressure, while the effect of air wherever it be is warmth, freshness and absence of pressure. This name and these effects are, in fact, the result of the penetrating one and not of the object of penetration, even though a summary consideration does not make a distinction between the two. On this account we said that the penetrating one is the determiner and the maintainer, while the object of penetration is the substratum and the matter. Afterwards we recognise a common factor between water and air, and that is the material form. The ascendance of both, the penetrating and the penetrated, unavoidably ends in two things. The first (material form) we call the Universal Soul and the second (object of penetration) the Rahmani Soul, (hyula).[1]

Sat' 3

The Universal Soul descended into a genus, a species and an individual, while the Rahmani Soul descended after its (Universal Soul's) descent. It is so because every form has a matter peculiar to it, while what is common (in the form and the matter) we have named Shakhs Akbar and its two parts have been named the Universal Soul and the matter, so that every detailed account which may be given should be attributed to its own origin.

When we look at the procession of consequences (Athar) we call Shakhs Akbar a Universal nature and every other soul (Nafs) a Particular nature. From these Particular souls the one which is nearest to abstraction (Tajarrud) is named "the world of spirits" and that which is remotest from abstraction is called "the visible

[1] Hyula has no name and it is the form that bears the names which change by the change of forms; and the properties are also meant for the form. The material form penetrating matter is called the Universal Soul, while the matter is named the Rahmani Soul.

world", while that which is the intermediate is termed "the world of similitude" (*Alam-i-mithal*).[1]

Sat' 4

When we place a date-stone in earth, and water and air enter into its (date-stone's) body, a power appears from it which absorbs the small parts of elements, and then transforms them into a form suitable to its own species. At that time, leaves come out and branches appear till the tree becomes complete.

Now if we think over it, we come to know two things. One is the tree-soul which by means of the date-stone has overflowed and the other is the materiality (*Jismaniyya*) which flows through shape, colour, lines, taste, odour, heat and cold, etc. Both of these meet together coincidentally in the small parts of the elements. One is the form which has penetrated them and the other are the accidents subsisting through them. Similarly, when seminal fluid settles in the womb of a female its predication is like the predication of the date-stone.

The existence of materiality by which one species becomes distinguished from other species is, however, quite clear. The tree-soul is established (*Mutahaqqiq*) from this point, that if this materiality were to change and be transformed a thousand times, this individual (tree) still remains the same as it originally was. Thus, the secret of the relation of this individual is something other than the materiality.

On the basis of this introduction, it should be remembered that there is a connection between every soul and materiality suitable to it, by which it is recognised as belonging to such-and-such species. But whence comes this connection? One should think over this rather deeply.

Sat' 5

The origin of this connection and this specification is

[1] The requirement of the Universal nature is called the Universal expediency, while the requirement of the Particular soul is termed the Particular expediency.

firmly fixed in Primal Providence. There He (God) has bound every substantial form with suitable accidental forms in fraternity, and has made them embrace each other. God in the stage of intellect made this fraternity binding according to the requirement of substances and accidents. Now this cannot be questioned as to "why?" It cannot be said as to why fire is hot and water is cold. Plain investigation requires that non-material pure spirits (*Mujarradat-i-mufariqa*) have secret relation with some matters and materiality. One can become the nest of the other. And these same relations can become the cause of the particular movement and the attribute of every celestial body. Philosophers are compelled to confirm these relations whether they understand them or not.

Afterwards when the empyrean heaven (*Falak al-Aflak*) was created, God placed the power of imagination in it, so that it might be a medium between the universals and the particulars. That power then became the nest of that relation. Its origin, however, was firmly fixed in the Divine Providence.

We can prove its being the nest by two examples; and they are as follows:

(1) As man is said to be composed of four elements, his humours have been divided into four kinds. Bile became the nest of the power of fire, Phlegm became the nest of the power of water and so on.

(2) If we count numbers in our intellect and then place before ourselves a line of pearls according to those numbers in the external world, one number would be opposite to one pearl, two opposite to two, three opposite to three, and so on. This intellectual form which is a secondary concept (*M'aqulat-i-thaniyya*) has taken some kind of existing thing in the external world in its nest, and has established a relation with it.

Sat' 6

The imaginative faculty flowed from the greatest of bodies (empyrean heaven) on to every celestial body and on every creature of earthly body possessing will. It is the case, therefore, that both man and animal have the faculty of imagination, where ideas (*M'aani*) put on the dress of materiality, and consequently matters (*Ajsam*) and materiality come out in the form of those ideas. There are, however, connections between those ideas and those material forms, conformable to the origin of the Divine (Primal) Providence. Thus, the form of a stone that comes into our intellectual faculty is different from that of a tree. Again when we see what was once forgotten, we recognise with certainty that it is that same thing which was forgotten. At the time of seeing, the thing is perceptible while at the time of its absence it is something imagined. The interpretation of dreams depends upon the knowledge of these connections. He who knows these connections better is better skilled in the interpretation.

Sometimes, a reflection of the imaginative form of the celestial spheres falls upon an element which is easily changeable and can assume different shapes, like air and the thing existing in the atmospheric world. Then on account of the flow of imagination on that matter, the earthly causes come into action and the form suitable to that imagination makes for an appearance in the visible world.

At times the reflection of the form imagined by the celestial spheres falls upon some materiality with the result that a picture appears there, either by the earthly causes coming into action or by effecting such contraction or expansion in them (causes) as may conform to the imagined thing. This faculty of imagination is of two kinds, and they are as follows:

(1) The imaginative (*Khiyaliyya*) faculty, corresponding to the shapes and the colours of bodies.

(2) The faculty of fancy (*Wahmiyya*), corresponding to particular ideas.

Again, it should be known that Shakhs Akbar combines everything, whether it be the greatest of bodies which in the terminology of philosophers is called the empyrean heaven, or the other celestial spheres, the Sublime Assembly, the Lower Assembly of the angels, or the species of animals. All of them are replete with the similitudinary faculty (*Quwwat-i-mithaliyya*), as if it (the similitudinary faculty) had filled the whole of the Universe. One covering is the soul and the other is the materiality, and the similitudinary faculty has fallen between these two.

Sat' 7

There is a fixed part in Shakhs Akbar which combines all the parts of the universe. It is finer, resembles more the Incorporeal (*Mujarrad*) and is more suitable to become its mirror. That part unifies Shakhs Akbar's faculties of fancy and imagination, because the similitudinary faculty is distinguished from other parts of the universe by virtue of its being the mirror of every idea and every form. The similitudinary faculty of Shakhs Akbar is nearest to the world of Divinity, and the part that unifies fancy and imagination bears relation to both idea and form. In short, this part became the mirror of the pure Incorporeal, as a polished body fallen in the desert is able by its own particular capability to become a mirror for the shining sun. The real cause of the particularisation of this part for becoming a mirror for the Real (*Haqq*) is the Divine Providence, where "why" is out of the question. Again, there is an attribute in this part and an attribute in the Real, just as we have explained the attribution of the incorporeal to some parts of the universe.[1]

Sat' 8

Just as an apparent form in the mirror has two aspects, by one it shows the perfection of the mirror, and by the other it reveals the form of the person looking into it; and

[1] The fixed part is particularised by its being the nest, while it is an attribute of the Real to have created it as such. Thus the attribute of the Real is active while that of the part is passive.

just as in our intellect the form of man has two aspects, one shows the perfection of our mind (*Nafs*) and the external existence of what occurs to it and the other shows the form of man. And the man on account of this form became intellectually existent and emerged from an absolute non-existence; similarly the form of the Real which appeared in the mirror of the fine part of Shakhs Akbar has also two aspects. One shows the perfection of Shakhs Akbar, counted as a universe, while the other shows the Real and Its existence.

This Divine Secret is a link between the Incorporeal and the visible world, as in one respect it is an abstract (*Mujarrad*) form, the appearance of the Real, and a pure incorporeality which does not admit of any matter, and in the other respect is reckoned as a mirror for the universe and is the best universe.

On that account it becomes an intermediary between the Incorporeal and the visible world. It is the Divine Manifestation in general, and every other manifestation is the manifestation of this manifestation.

Sa't 9

God is both the suppressor (*Qabidh*) and the expander (*Basit*). He suppresses some of the causes with the result that an extremely trifling and mean effect comes into existence. He expands some of the causes and thus an extremely great and magnificent effect emerges. He has effected a great expansion in the appearance of this form in this mirror. The maker of the forms (God) has made this form a pretext for the execution of His commands (*Ahkam*), and has made this a means for the completion of His own works, so that His name in the apparent form in the mirror creates an impression different from the intended one. It is so because a certain meaning which is not actually meant quickly occurs to the understanding of the hearers. The nearest of words which completely suits the meaning is the second appearance; and the nearest example of the connection of the Incorporeal with the visible words by means of this secret is the connection the human soul (*Nafs-i-Natiga*) has with the body by means of a spirit (*Ruh*) poured into the heart. Again the nearest example of this Divine Secret in the emanation of actions and their attribution to the Pure Incorporeal is afforded by the movement of fingers in our saying "Zaid has necessarily to move his fingers so long as he is writing" in the sense that both the writer and the quality of writing have to act simultaneously when the fingers have necessarily to move.

When a gnostic reaches this Divine Appearance (*Dhurur*) and looks intently at it, he sees in it only an incorporeality. The mirror does not come to his sight at all, nay even its presence does not occur to his mind. It is just like this, that when we see our form in the mirror, the mirror drops out of this observation and we become negligent of it, whether we like it or not. God forbid! if the eye were to fall upon the mirror, we should fall from the stage of knowledge to that of ignorance and from the stage of acquaintance to that of non-acquaintance. Therefore there is absolutely no mention of this mirror in the mines of knowledge (*Hadirat al-Quds*) lying by the side of the extensive realms of Divinity. Unavoidably, those tongues (Prophets) which are the interpreters of the Real find no other word than the Divine Manifestation, the Second Appearance and their like. Try to understand this point and do not speak of it again.

Sat' 10

When we think of a spherical object, it becomes necessary that it should have a centre, and when we think of that spherical object as moving, it becomes necessary that it should have a circumference, a diameter and an axis.[1] Similarly, when God in the stage of intellect

[1] Whenever one thinks of a spherical object, he will have necessarily to think of its necessaries. The universe, namely the Great Body, is from the necessaries of God in the stage of intellect. Thus, he who thinks of God will have necessarily to think of the universe.

required the existence of the universe, this requirement for the universe led by way of necessity to a particular requirement, which is capable of the appearance of the Great Manifestation. After that, the capability of the agent (*Fa'il*) and the patient (*Qabil*) became the cause of the necessary appearance of that manifestation in it. The real truth about the Great Manifestation is this point, but as the action of the wise is not devoid of wisdom, many effects beyond computation resulted from the existence of the Great Manifestation both in the Divine plane and in the plane of possible existence. What we have mentioned before is the knowledge (*M'arifat*) of the Great Manifestation in relation to a cause which required it from above. Now we desire to explain the effects resulting from the existence of the Great Manifestation (*Tajalli Azam*), so that its reality may be made completely clear.

Sat' 11

By means of this manifestation the renewed intention (*Iradah mutajaddah*) is proved for God, but this intention is other than the one a philosopher calls the very person of God, and is also different from the one a dialectician takes pains to prove. An elucidation of this summary is this, that to shed light is necessary for the sun which lasts as long as the sun lasts; but there happens to be a particular kind of effect of light on a particular body at one time but not at other times because of a temporary condition. Thus at mid-day it makes the stone hot and at another time causes the ice to melt. In this way, the action of light becomes renewed, lasting as long as the sun lasts. In fact, the cause of this renewal is earthly capabilities and to this same knowledge (*M'arifat*) a reference has been made in the Word of God "Every day He is in a new splendour".[1]

Again, this point may be understood that the creation

---

[1] Qur'an, Surah Al-Rahman, V. 29.

of certain capabilities takes place in the World of Divinity, and the created thing by the grace of Reality (God) becomes a spirituality of the event there, or its essential form, "say what you like".[1] Those certain capabilities are the result of the conjunctions of the powers of celestial spheres in some particular way in the general conjunctions. That spirituality is a similitudinary form of that event in the natural faculties of the celestial spheres. There is a reference to this knowledge in the Word of God "Verily We have sent it down in a blessed night, in (night) is made distinct every affair of wisdom, by command from Our presence. For We (ever) send 'relevations' ".[2]

Thereafter this meaning excited the causes of pleasure, hatred and ambition in the minds of the Exalted Assembly and those of the lower one. "Those who bear the Throne and those around it are singing (His) glory."[3] After that the angels had to wait for an appointed term as was specified by the Divine Wisdom for the execution of that spirituality on the earth. "When their appointed term is reached, not an hour can they cause delay nor (an hour) can they advance (it in anticipation)."[4] When the appointed term comes, the angels of God become the servants of that spirituality and prepare the earth for its descent. God has said "And We have sent down iron",[5] and "He has sent down cattle".[6]

After all this, when this spirituality descends on earth and produces a particular effect, then the condition obtained happens to resemble the condition of an occurrence of an intention in the minds of creatures possessing the power of will. On that account, in Law,

---

[1] From here is known that for every created thing, there is a spirituality which is named as 'Ayn-i-thabitah, the fixed prototype or latent reality.

[2] Qur'an, Surah Al-Dukhan, V. 3–5.

[3] Ibid. Al-Mumin, V. 7.

[4] Ibid. Yunus, V. 49.

[5] Ibid. Al-Hadid, V. 25.

[6] Ibid. Al-Zumar, V. 6.

the name of this Divine attribute is the Will (*Irada*); because the Will at its very outset means an appearance of the intellectual form of the thing. After that, an admiration for and an inclination towards it takes place. That inclination then mixes with the temper of the heart, and this is how resolution emerges. Thereafter, the bodily powers follow that resolution, just as you have come to know of these stages in the Will of God. There is His saying "And when We wish to destroy a town We (first) send a definite order there to those who are given the good things of this life".[1] "When He wills a thing, His command is 'Be' and it is."[2]

Sat' 12

If you want to know by way of an ocular demonstration how the predication (*Hukm*) of the Great Manifestation penetrates the universe, then think upon a grain of pulse, every part of which is connected with the other part. When you throw it into water, the water gradually runs through every part of it, so that the form of pulse does not disappear or differ from what it originally was, and there is a natural increase in all directions. The place of its every part in connection and relation to the other part, however, remains the same as it originally was. Similar is the case in the universe where all the heavenly and earthly causes, as well as the causes of will of creatures possessing the power of will, are following their natural course. Every cause is connected with its effect. Just as the moisture of water has penetrated every part, similarly a fresh light from the Great Manifestation has permeated every cause and effect,[3] and has removed every cause from its real causality and instead has made its apparent causality remain. The fire according to the apparent cause is to burn cotton, but in reality both the

---

[1] Surah Bani Israil, V. 16.
[2] Ibid. Yasin, V. 82.
[3] By means of similitudinary power which is present everywhere.

burning of fire and cotton's being burnt are attributed to this Great Manifestation. All causes and effects are from action under the power of this light. This is the meaning you have heard in Shariat that the real agent is God and all other causes are working according to the usual course. For explaining this meaning, no clearer words can be found.

Sat' 13

By means of this Manifestation it is proved that God possesses a power other than the one which philosophers term the very essence of Divinity, and also different from the power which dialecticians represent as equal to human faculties. An explanation of this summary is this, that when both the heavenly and the earthly causes become fully ripe, a ray radiating from the Great Manifestation falls upon the Sublime Assembly, the Lower Assembly and upon the creatures possessing will (*Irada*). That ray then becomes the cause of the administration of the desired work through the suppression of some causes, the expansion of others and by inspiring certain creatures. Consequently all these angels and the inspired creatures which are the armies of God come into action until that desired form spreads on the earth. Thus there appears an attribute from the obedience of the world to this ray. This has been made clear in these words of God: "And God has full power and control over His affairs",[1] "To God belongs the Kingdom of the heavens and the earth",[2] "And He has power to send calamities on you, from above and below or to cover you with confusion in party strife".[3]

Sat' 14

By means of this Manifestation is proved God's know-

[1] Qur'an, Surah Yusuf, V. 21.
[2] Ibid. Al-Ma'idah, V. 17.
[3] Ibid. Al-Anam, V. 65.

ledge and His sense of hearing and seeing. All these are actual attributes of God; not in the sense in which the philosophers call them the very essence of God and also not in the sense in which the dialecticians speak of the Essential attributes. An elucidation of this summary is that for the Great Manifestation is proved a pure and co-present relation with all the parts of the universe, whether higher or lower, and with every leaf, every drop of rain and with every piece of stone.

"A connection without any adaptation and beyond all comprehension,
The Lord of mankind has with both the Genii and men."

It is so because the relation of the Abstract pure with the whole of the universe is one and the same. If we were to consider this relation in connection with visible objects it is seeing, and consider it in connection with the audible it is hearing, and take it into consideration in connection with things other than these two, it is knowledge. Thus, this Great Manifestation by way of this connection is near to every particle. If its (the particle's) survival is intended it (the Great Manifestation) makes it survive and if its destruction is desired it destroys it or changes it from one state to another state. Thus, it is its guardian, its inspector, the knower of its affairs, the hearer of its words and the seer of its essence (*Dhat*). This is the language of the Qur'an, as knowledge has been confined to these three kinds, namely, the ears, the eyes and the heart. In many verses the direction is given in this language and from this the meaning of "guardian" and "witness over everything" becomes clear.

Sat' 15

Legislation (*Tashri'a*) is the complement of predestination (*Taqdir*).[1] By predestination is meant that for every

[1] Fuller explanation of this Sat' is found in *Hujjatullah al-Balighah*, in the chapter on *Inshiqaqu-ut-Taklif min at-Taqdir*.

species a constitution, certain manners and actions are fixed. Man for example is the speaking one, understanding speech, is smooth of skin, straight in stature and walking on two feet; while the horse is the neighing one, unable to understand speech, hairy of skin, with a curved stature and walking on four feet. At a time of anger it bites and kicks with its legs, while the bull butts with its horns. At the time of mounting a female, every species has particular movements, different from the movements of other species. Similarly at the time of eating, drinking and rearing its young, etc., the way of one species differs from that of another. All this flows on creatures possesssing will (*Irada*) through natural instincts.

By legislation is meant that as man is composed of two faculties, the angelic and the bestial, his specific equilibrium requires such proceedings by means of which both the faculties may remain where they are in their normal condition, and in the other world happiness should be his share. And in the necessary workings of life (*Irtifaqat*), namely in the ways of living, marriage, seeking of livelihood and in the administration of cities, he should not go outside the straight road.

The regulation of all these affairs and works for the species of man is in other words the Legislation. The case is like this, that the Great Manifestation gives a summary gaze at the human form with the result that many sparks strike out between it and this human form. What it signifies is this, that man is ordered to do certain actions and on doing them depends the pleasure of God, whether those actions be necessary or recommendatory; and he is prohibited from doing certain actions and on doing them depends His displeasure, whether those actions be unlawful or reprehensible. From this ethical science appeared. God says: "The word does not change before Me".[1] After that on certain occasions and times and with certain persons and people this same summary science becomes detailed in this manner, that people should

[1] Qur'an, Surah Qaf, V. 29.

discharge those universal affairs in such-and-such a way. The reference to the first is given in the verse: "He has established the same religion for you as He enjoined on Noah",[1] while the reference to the second is made in the verse, "To each among you We have prescribed a Law and an Open way".[2]

Sat' 16

God gave an intentive look into the human form and observed the properties and actions of the species. All those sciences, beliefs and the moral character by which the normal condition of the species could be realised sparked out from this look. And from there the seven sciences became represented in the Holy Fold (*Hadhirat al-Quds*). Those sciences are as follows:

(1) Theology (*'Ilm ilahiyat*): This may be acquired to the extent that the belief in it is the cause of an improvement of the normal condition of the species. By theology man knows the attributes of God which are proved only by means of the Great Manifestation.

(2) Natural sciences (*'Ilm tabi'aiyat*): Here a physicist thinks over these sciences in one way, and a follower of the Qur'an thinks in some other way. For example, a physicist thinks over the animals in order to know the properties of every species, a prince thinks over them just to know which animal is fit for riding and which one is suitable for carrying a load. The follower of the Qur'an looks at those species only to understand the Divine power, its knowledge and its wisdom. This science is called a reminder of the Signs of God.

(3) The science of the Days of God, namely, the events which happened in consequence of giving reward to the obedient and punishment to the disobedient.

(4) The science of the Day of Resurrection, Paradise and Hell.

---

[1] Qur'an, Surah Al-Shura, V. 13.
[2] Ibid. Al-Ma'idah, V. 48.

(5) The science of Disputation. Disputations were held with those who had gone astray. In the Holy Qur'an, the Disputation has been confined to four groups, namely, the Polytheists, the Jews, the Christians and the Hypocrites.

(6) The science of the five Commandments: Obligatory (*Wajib*), Recommended (*Mandub*), Permissible (*Mubah*), Reprehensible (*Makruh*) and Forbidden (*Haram*). This science also discusses the properties of actions done in the household economy, the rulership of cities, the manners of living and spiritual morals.

(7) An event occurs by which a Persuasion (*Targhib*) or Intimidation (*Tarhib*) is intended, or a threat to people who lag or admiration for those who are prompt in the acts of obedience is desired, so that the intended object may be achieved. Thus, what is desired is revealed. This seventh science, however, stands in need of the "Occasion of Revelation".

Sat' 17

One of the Divine attributes is to give such teaching to the servant which may be proper for him. Such teaching is of various kinds, and they are as follows:

(1) Through the natural instincts which spark out in the perceptive faculty and in times of need by means of the specific form. God says: "And Thy Lord inspired the bee".[1]

(2) By inspiring something in the mind wherein lies the good of the person without his being conscious of it. God says: "And We inspired the mother of Moses: 'Suckle him (thy child)'."[2] This sparks out in the perceptive faculty and the unexpected capability he acquires at that time by means of celestial powers or through the angels who are the servants of the secret of creation.

[1] Qur'an, Surah Al-Nahl, V. 68.
[2] Ibid. Al-Qasas, V. 7.

(3) By occasioning thoughts: These are thoughts which spark out in the mind of man in his permanent states (*Muqamat*). Thoughts such as those of pleasure, submission, patience, intention, repentance, abstinence, love, conviction and so on. And also the thoughts which spark out in his nature by means of his dominating concentration upon Divinity.

(4) Through discernment (*Firasat*): This sparks out in the mind of man by means of an imagination (*Wahm*) when he sees something and certain bodies existing in the external world. This is just like the sparking of fear in the heart of a goat when it sees a wolf or its form.

(5) By means of a dream: It is a representation of knowledge in the form of thoughts when the senses cease functioning and the man reacts towards those thoughts as they actually were in the external world. Some dreams are real which the angel inspires, their pattern is after the pattern of inspiration in the second sense.[1] Some dreams are angelic, and by this is meant the representation of the angelic attributes which appear in man in suitable forms. For example, a man who observes purity may see himself as shining. And some dreams are, however, only a confused medley of thoughts.

(6) The strongest of the Divine teaching is the revelation to the prophets with particular meaning. There are, however, many reasons accounting for the difference between revelation and inspiration, and they are as follows:

i. In the case of revelation, first of all, the perceptive faculties of the person concerned are suppressed by the faculties of the Sublime Assembly, and then afterwards, the knowledge flows towards him from the Holy Fold. In inspiration both these things are wanting.

ii. In every created thing there is certainly a capacity for being a patient (*Qabil*, lit. 'in a condition to') to accept the effect of the agent (*Fa'il*). Now when the capacity of a particular person is found ready to receive teaching,

---

[1] By this is meant the "inspiration into the mind".

then that (teaching) is inspiration; but if a general
Universal administration (of the Holy Fold) precedes in
the preparation of this flow outside the capacity of a
particular person, then that is revelation.

iii. Revelation is far away from the ambiguity of the
confused medley of dreams, is free from mistake in its
interpretation and is immune from error in the understanding of the intended meaning. It is so because the
will of God is to establish the good of the world, and this
will of God is not given up at any time. God says: "Nor
will He disclose to you the secrets of the Unseen, but He
chooses of His Apostles (for this purpose) whom He
pleases".[1] On this account, the revelation of the prophets
is a certain science, whether it be through discernment,
dream or inspiration into the mind. It is not like the
inspiration of the saints (*Awliyya*, lit. 'friends'), their
dream and the unseen voice they sometimes hear. Do not
make the mistake here of considering the thoughts of
saints as equal to revelation. Many an error for the people
of these times has arisen out of this mistake.

Sat' 18

It has been proved through veridical vision that the
time the Universal Soul (*Nafs-i-Kull*) happens to become
a human soul, and that mostly takes place when it is
puffed into an embryo, the form of the Great Body
becomes concealed in that human soul, and a point
opposite to each one of the heavenly and the earthly
bodies is also kept concealed in it. If the Sun or Venus
happens to be at its Zenith at that moment in the external world, a point opposite to that Sun and that Venus
is also placed in it. And in this way a specimen of all the
things of heaven and earth remains concealed in that
soul. This subject needs detailing, but there is no scope
for that in this treatise.

In short, a specimen of the Great Manifestation and of
the Holy Fold, which is the place of the reflection of its

[1] Qur'an, Surah Al-Imran, V. 178.

rays, is placed in the soul of man. In some it is clear and
manifest, while in others it is dim and misty. If it is clear
and manifest then this person is perfect. In our terminology that point which is a specimen of the Great
Manifestation is called the Pure Intellect serving as a
mirror.

Its example in relation to the Great Manifestation is
like the example of a mirror fallen on the ground. When
the sun reaches directly opposite to it, its form actually
appears in it, and when it is not quite opposite to it, only
radiance appears in that mirror, and not its form. But
when the mirror is broken into pieces, nothing save a
kind of whiteness appears in those parts. In like manner,
the Pure Intellect varies in human souls. A soul in which
the actual form of Divinity appears bold is a perfect man,
and so on and on till the turn of the mystics comes.[1]

Sat' 19

One of the actions proceeding from the Great Manifestation to the universe is the descent of an intention for
the guidance of human beings, for giving them teaching
of the knowledge of the Origin and the future life, and
for explaining to them the ways of seeking nearness to
God. This intention at times descends for keeping away
the accursed group of beings from men or for removing
acts of injustice from among them or for delivering them
from destructive acts like the preparation of the boat of
Noah; and other examples of such significance are
intended. After that the Divine Administration (*Tadbir-
i-Ilahi*) which is based on the selection of the fittest (for
survival) becomes confined, on that day, to taking a
perfect person from among men as a tool, and then
through him getting the desired object achieved.[2] Thus

---

[1] The mystics in their spiritual progress do not see the Great
Manifestation as it actually is, but rather its spreading rays.

[2] The perfect man, namely the prophet, believes and is convinced
that this mission is his, and he, therefore, does not hesitate in
staking his life for its fulfilment.

94

that intention actually gets imprinted in his Pure Intellect as the reflection of the form of the sun gets imprinted in the mirror. At that time both the spiritual and the intellectual faculties of that person become bright by the light of the Pure Intellect with the result that many (Divine) sciences and countless intentions descend upon him, and he gains a wonderful relation with the Sublime Assembly. The science of the Law and philosophy are poured on his heart with great abundance. This is how the Divine Administration gets the desired work done by him, and the name of this dear one is the Apostle.

Here it is necessary to note one point. Even if the Messenger acquires some sciences through a dream or discernment, as their source is the Pure Intellect they are unavoidably definite and certain and never admit of any change, alteration, doubt or suspicion whatsoever. God says: "He sends His angels with inspiration of His command to such of His servants as He pleases, (saying): 'Warn (men) that there is no god but I: so do your duty unto Me'.[1] And He, raised high above the ranks of the Lord of the Throne, says, 'By His command does He send the spirit (of inspiration) to any of His servants He pleases, that he may warn (men) of the Day of Mutual Meeting, the Day whereon they will (all) come forth. Not a single thing concerning them is hidden from God. Whose will be the Dominion that Day? That of God, the One, the Irresistible'."[2]

Sat' 20

At times the Will of God is connected with this object, that the Guidance should remain with people for ever, and that they should hold fast to the rope of God generation after generation, and that both the near and the far should equally draw near it. Consequently the Divine grace subjugates the mind of the Apostle and summarily

[1] Qur'an, Surah Al-Nahl, V. 2.
[2] Ibid. Al-Mu'min, V. 15–16.

pours the Book of God into his Pure Intellect. That form which appeared in the Holy Fold appears in it (Pure Intellect) as well. On this account definite knowledge is gained that it is the Word of God. After that, a well-arranged speech is poured down time after time in his intellectual faculties through the angels. God says: "With it came down the Spirit of Faith and Truth to thy heart and mind, that you may admonish".[1] In this state stream after stream of the Divine grace from the fountains of mercy flows towards him; and that revealed thing is the "Book of God".

The Jinn subjugates the minds of the soothsayers and inspires in them certain sciences, while the minds of the prophets are subjugated by angels of higher ranks, and here the inspiration of sciences comes from the Great Manifestation. It is just like the concealment of water in damp air which (air) in turn turns the cloth damp.

Sat' 21

God knew in the Primal Providence (*Ghaib al-Ghaib*) that in such-and-such a period of time people would stand in need of Guidance. And the most suitable plan at that time would be to send a perfect man possessing a strongly effective Pure Intellect. A man for whom, according to the heavenly plan, good luck and the ability to prevail over the people of his time, and according to the earthly plan, the possession of both the intellectual and practical faculties in such a state of equilibrium as to become a vehicle for the specific form in the best possible manner, had already been decided. God also knew that stream after stream of blessings from the Great Manifestation should reach his Pure Intellect, and the revelation of the Qur'an should also be the result of the perfection of the self of that dear one, and also a sign of the fulfilment of the rights on the part of the

[1] Qur'an, Surah Al-Shu'ara, V. 193-94.

Great Manifestation itself. He also knew that the Messenger should be an Arab, and as the Arabs were to be addressed, it is but necessary that the Qur'an should be revealed in the Arabic language. God says: "What a foreign (tongue) and an Arab!"[1] Again, if the people are found interested in the show of eloquence, and the speech (word of God) be not extraordinarily eloquent, it will not prove effective among them. It is, therefore, necessary that the Qur'an should be revealed in a style which may be neither poetry nor prose, neither a dialogue nor an epistle, so that it may be a strong defence against their thoughts. He represented all these points in the style of the Qur'an, and represented the secret of Legislation (*Tashri'a*) in its revealed meanings. Thus, all this became represented in the Holy Fold and was taken into account from the lights, the explanation and the elucidation of the Great Manifestation.

Sat' 22

The Divine blessings descend upon the heart of the Apostle from two sources. The first source is the ocean of legislation as I have already explained the truth of its seven sciences (in Sat' 16). The second source is the ocean of the secret of the Speech and the formal specification, whence the Qur'an is revealed to his heart. Now, if the first source were to recede and the second one to precede, then that is a Divine Tradition. But if the source of Speech were to precede and that of Legislation to recede, then it is likely it may not take place. All the Divine books which were revealed before the Qur'an were revealed after the type of the Divine Tradition save what God pleased, and on that account the Holy Prophet has said, "Only that thing used to be revealed to the prophet in the like of which people had already believed".

Two things are necessary to a Divine book, and they are:

[1] Qur'an, Surah Al-Nahl, V. 103.

(1) The Divine blessings are showered upon those people and the Sublime Assembly shows its pleasure and admiration for them who read that Book and work for the dissemination of its teachings.

(2) That Book is to survive for ever, and the Community will also receive the Divine support to preserve it. If these two things were to be found wanting, then that would not be a Book of God, but rather a scroll of a human being who by his own intention collected the knowledge of his Apostle, like the collection of the Sahih of Bukhari and the Sahih of Muslim in our Community.

Sat' 23

If we say that the Gulistan (of Saadi) is written on leaves of paper, is read by the tongues of children and is preserved in their hearts, came into existence five hundred years back and its author is Shaikh Saadi, then this is all correct, because the verification of each one of these statements is implied in the existence of another, namely that it is written in the form of handwriting, is read in the form of letters, is preserved in the form of intellect, is the composition of Shaikh Saadi in the respect that the arrangement of those words is the work of his intellectual faculty and that five hundred years have passed since the (appearance of the) Gulistan itself. These usages are, however, current in all books in every language both in ancient and modern times. On the analogy of these usages, you understand that the Qur'an is written in books, is read by tongues, is preserved in our hearts, and the speaker of it is God. Add (to these) the other usage also that it is eternal, because its one form was already there in existence in the Eternal Providence (*'Inayat-i-Azliyya*) before the existence of the universe.

Sat' 24

It has been known by veridical vision that every individual who comes into the visible world has to go through a cyclical process. In the beginning he was an abstract, pure intellect. When the appointed time comes, he comes to the visible world from the place which is the most superior imaginative creation (*Nisha'at*). The way of his first appearance is that the Abstract pure, in relation to its own specification, draws his similitudinary picture in the similitudinary world and in the faculties of the celestial spheres and those of the Sublime Assembly. At that time it is said: "God has written what has happened and what is to happen", and that drawn picture is called "the clear writing" and "the guarded tablet". After that, he enters into the various stages of the World of Similitude. The earthly causes are then made obedient to his appearance and a fixed time is specified for it (his appearance) in the material world. When that fixed time comes he appears in the material form and completes the duration of his life. Thereafter, the material form separates from the earthly parts and he stays on the perceptive faculties of both the celestial spheres and the Sublime Assembly. After that, he ascends through the same process he had descended from till he reaches the same point. At that time, he throws off the unclean form from himself and becomes the same pure intellect he originally was.

Sat' 25

When men die a natural death, they still retain with themselves as great a portion of their natural spirits as could be a steed for the Soul and remain in the Intermediary World (*'Alam-i-barzakh*) retaining the knowledge, the states and the faculties which remained imprinted upon their natural spirits. The man then becomes like a rider whose horse has been taken away from him, or like a writer whose hands have been cut off. This is the same human being with his constitution and attributes save that his hands and feet are broken off. He, however, sees as one sees in a dream, with his own intellectual faculties the approval and the disapproval of the Sublime Assembly and imagines pictures of pleasing and unpleasing happenings. It is wonderful that some similitudinary faculties are opened upon men, as has come in the Tradition "The souls of martyrs are in the bellies of green birds".

Here it is proper to understand one point. In the worldly life the natural faculties of man according to his natural disposition are turned towards the visible world, because the mainstay of his living is eating and drinking. In the Intermediary World the attention of his intellectual and practical faculties is drawn towards the Similitudinary World, mostly towards its restricted form which constitutes his imaginative faculty.[1] He sees his firmly-settled faculties in the form of imagination or fancy, and this is what the nature of the Intermediary World also requires. Sometime his attention is diverted towards the Absolute Similitudinary World, but this, however, depends on the capability of an individual. At times, the angels of the lower rank put in charge of the spirits are inspired by the Sublime Assembly to deal with the buried one with gentleness or with violence. The buried one understands their dealing and sees them in the similitudinary forms, and knows them as commanded by God. In short, he continues in this state of dream right up to the Day of the Last Judgment.

Sat‘ 26

When the other appointed term comes, the similitudinary faculties enter into the spirits by way of necessity, because of the individual's having gone through the various stages of Similitude. There he will see through the absolute similitudinary form those of his deeds and character which were preserved, and will find the approval or the disapproval of the Sublime Assembly

[1] The Similitudinary World is of two kinds, the absolute and the restricted. The light of the sun which falls on the ground is however, restricted, as it is present in one place and absent in the other. But when we see it in the sky above, it is absolute.

as the case may be. Both the Guidance and the Scheme (*Tadbir*) of God working in the universe will appear there in the similitudinary form. Many persons here will have one and the same perception, because the line of the specific form is one and the scheme of the similitudinary faculties is also one. Many individual characteristics (*Ahkam*) which were borne by the Nasmic, terrestrial human faculties will disappear here. This day is called the "Day of Mutual Meeting". "Raised high above ranks the Lord of the Throne sends by His command the spirit (of inspiration) to any one of His servants He pleases, that he may warn (men) of the Day of Mutual Meeting, the Day whereon they will (all) come forth. Not a single thing concerning them is hidden from God."[1]

In this place, the Reckoning, the Balance, the Fountain and the things like the Scroll and the Bridge will come into appearance. Here the Great Manifestation will appear in a similitudinary form worthy of its rank, a form in which it had never appeared in the world at any time nor had it ever occurred to the mind of any one. People will see it openly and the complete mercy flowing from the fountain of goodness will descend on them.[2] And all the necessary things of life like eating, drinking, dressing and having intercourse will take certain forms, because all these were the requirements of the human form and not the peculiarity of one individual or the other. They will find pleasure in each one of them. Every pleasure refers to a certain act of goodness which they had taken care to look after; and in everything they will clearly see themselves as satisfied with their character, beliefs and actions.

On the Day of "Mutual Meeting" many human beings will take their bodies, the origin of which was, however, preserved even though to a very small extent (to the extent of the root of the tail) as a vehicle for their souls.

---

[1] Qur'an, Surah Al-Mu'min, V. 15–16
[2] By the fountain of goodness is meant the Sublime Assembly and the Holy Fold.

This will not be in the way it was in the beginning, but for the purpose that it may serve as a mirror for the similitudinary predications (*Ahkam*), so that the length of the neck of the crier to prayer (*Mu'adhdhin*), the whiteness of the face of the happy, the eating and drinking may be clearly represented. All this will take place by way of necessity, because of man's having passed through the various stages of the Similitude. When the elemental life is destroyed, it is but necessary that this individual should come under the similitudinary faculties, and there the similitudinary predications will make their appearance exactly.

Sat' 27

The souls of the perfect individuals in which the Pure Intellect shines brightly are like a mirror placed in front of the sun wherein its form is actually reflected. So long as they are in the world, they are the servants of the Manifestation. A spark-like Universal cause spreads down from it (this Manifestation) and falls upon them like the falling of a spark on to cotton. In consequence, a particular attribute emerges. God said to Moses: "And I have chosen thee for Myself".[1]

When they (perfect individuals) go to the Intermediary World and throw off their bodily veil, the form of the sun prevails upon the whole of their minds. The point of the form of the sun remains as the main one and all the rest become redundant. After that, these minds are attracted time after time towards the Great Manifestation. Then it looks as if this form is the possessor of the form itself. This is how the branch is tied fast to its root. The meaning of heterogeneity is gone both intellectually and outside the intellect. The needle desires to be lost, while the thread inserted in its eye does not allow it.[2]

[1] Qur'an, Surah Taha, V. 41.
[2] By this thread is meant the "Nasmah" which, however, preserves otherness and does not permit becoming one.

This, however, is the state of the superior minds of the perfect. There the Great Manifestation also creates the Universal causes in these particular relative minds, and except through the interference of other minds, they do not become capable of reaching the earth. Besides these minds, there are other minds lesser in rank one after another till the turn of the pious (Abrar) comes who are like the light of the sun on earth without a veil or like the light under the veil of a cloud. This is the detailed account of perfect human minds.

Besides them there are Pure Intellects of the spirits of the celestial spheres and of the greatest angels nearest to the Throne of God who, possessing similar attributes, are the foremost among all these in this respect. In one respect they are absorbed and lost, and in another respect, they are sober and surviving, and so on and on till the turn of the Sublime Assembly comes which is made by the Universal scheme to influence the human species through the faculties of the common sense (Hiss-i-mushtarik, 'the undifferentiated perception') and the thought of an individual person, and has linked the order of their (human beings') life with that body (Sublime Assembly).[1]

God says: "Those who bear the throne of power and those around it celebrate the praise of their Lord and believe in Him and ask protection for those who believe. Our Lord, Thou embracest all things in mercy and knowledge, so protect those who turn (to Thee) and follow Thy way, and save them from the chastisement of hell. Our Lord, make them enter the Gardens of perpetuity, which Thou hast promised them and such of their fathers and their wives and offspring as are good. Surely Thou art the Mighty, the Wise. And guard them from evil, and whom Thou guardest from evil this day, Thou hast indeed mercy on him. And that is the mighty achievement."[2]

---

[1] The celestial spheres and the angels also possess Pure Intellects.
[3] Qur'an, Surah Al-Mu'min, V. 7-8.

Sat' 28

In Law (*Shar'a*) this assembled body is called the
exalted companion, the exalted council and the Holy
Fold. Their habitation is neither in the up nor in the
down but is the very heart and the mind of the Great
Body which has no connection whatsoever with any
direction. The thing which resembles the Holy Fold the
most is a ray round a sapphire, or a lamp placed in a
window. These spirits, even though they occupy different
positions in respect of the superiority of ranks, nearness
and close relation are, however, one and the same plane
externally, just as the rays of sapphire and lamp are one
and the same plane mutually connected.

It has been understood through veridical vision that
whenever any one spirit from them moves upwards, it
becomes necessary that some other spirit may be put in
its place, so that the plane should not be rent. "That is
the decree of (Him), the Exalted in Might, the All-
knowing."[1] Thus it is, therefore, that the change of
similars (*Amthal*, 'similitudes') always continues.

Sat' 29

The last move of the soul of the perfect is to disappear
in this Manifestation. The details of this summary are
that the Divine form which is the origin of all these souls
and is the most strong constituent of these points in relation to the essential unity, is the Great Manifestation
itself. As such, if the form of the sun were to appear in a
thousand mirrors, it could still be said to be one and the
same. Whatever difference is there, it is because of the
difference the souls have among themselves. The cause of
this difference is the connection of the soul with the
matter. In the beginning this matter was elemental, but
when the corporeal body separated (at the time of

[1] Qur'an, Surah Yasin, V. 38.

death) it (soul) became connected with the "Nasmic" body, and subsequently when the "Nasmic" body also began to disintegrate, then to whatever extent it disintegrated, the soul diverged from it correspondingly in respect of dependence and in turn became correspondingly dependent upon the plane of Similitude. The stages of Similitude are, however, different and manifold. The highest of these is this singular, simple point which is fixed in the whole of "Shakhs Akbar". It is unique and has no partner. The last natural ascent of the soul of the perfect is to reach this point. When matter reaches this point and the form appearing in the mirror becomes one with the Great Manifestation, this long journey comes to an end. Perfect and complete poverty (*Faqr*, 'humility of spirit') is indeed this.

Sat' 30

The souls of the happy, whose happiness has not reached absolute perfection, will have to hover around the Throne of Reality (God) for years.[1] "And you will see the angels hovering round the Throne."[2] It is then possible that, after undergoing many changes and states, they may succeed in losing themselves in Pure light. There are other particular souls as well the returning place of which is the specific form of man.[3] The specific form appears in different mirrors. The souls, in respect of human specific form, were one; and in respect of the different mirrors were many. But when mirrors—after passing through many changes, states, alteration of symbols (*Amthal*, 'similitudes') and the renewal of conditions—are destroyed, their multiplicity will also be automatically destroyed.

The Abstract human form is one of the bearers of the

[1] It refers to persons in whose hearts the Great Manifestation had not permanently settled.

[2] Qur'an, Surah Al-Zumar, V. 75.

[3] Namely, humanity. Those souls which are not attracted towards 'humanity' will, however, go to hell.

Throne.[1] In the renewal of similars and the change of conditions, its predication is like the predication of the bearers of the Throne. All these are the ranks of Paradise; some of them are however higher than others.

As regards the unhappy souls, between which and the Origin of the universe ignorance has set in, and which had met with much confusion in their going through the various states of the Similitude, they will be put into a strange perplexity, an explanation of which is rather lengthy.

Satᶜ 31

I am putting forward a simile which will become the key of some subtle sciences. Once a king of the world intended to arrange a feast, put on a rich garment, wear precious pearls on his body, adorn himself for his army, nay, for himself, increase his pleasure many times by various kinds of illumination and manifest his other forms of beauty. Accordingly he sent orders to all the countries under his rule that wherever they found land fit for the cultivation of sesame they should sow sesame there, and wherever a land be found suitable for the planting of walnut trees they should plant that tree there. Where they found wax, they should seize it, and where they found good fat they should purchase it. When this order reached the countries, their governors went in search of them. Wherever the land was found suitable for the cultivation of sesame and the planting of walnut trees, they seized it for the king and so improved

[1] The progress of man is by two ways. One way is to follow the path of prophecy (*Nubuwwat*), and the other way is to pursue the course of saintship (*Wilayat*). The man possesses Pure Intellect and the human soul (*Nafs-i-Natiqa*). If he progresses by means of the Pure Intellect he will reach the Great Manifestation, but in case his progress is made through the human and the angelic soul he will, however, reach 'humanity', and would be one of the bearers of the Throne. The former way is of prophecy while the latter one is of saintship. The most perfect one is he who combines both the ways.

it that no land other than that attributed to the king could show such improvement. Necessarily, they brought skilled cultivators and fat cattle and reserved a stream flowing brimful from the river for the supply of water to that land. These people with great anxiety and care prepared for the cultivation. When the field sown with sesame appeared blossoming and the garden of walnut trees also flourished, the superiority of that land to all the sown fields and gardens became manifest. Everyone, high and low, was saying: "The cultivation of the king and the garden of the king should be like this". In this case the address: "Had it not been for you, I would not have created the heavens," was directed to this cultivation and to this garden.

When the time of reaping the sesame and of gathering the walnuts came, all that cultivation and all those gardens were neglected. The address: "Had it not been for you, I would not have created the heavens" now became directed to the grains of sesame and to the harvest of walnuts. After that, they entrusted all this to the oil-presser. That skilled man, after a thorough search, separated the grains of sesame from every extraneous thing which was in them, pounded them and prepared a fine and pure essence. He then threw that essence in the oil pressing machine and brought out pure oil from it and ignored the rest. Then the address: "Had it not been for you, I would not have created the heavens" turned to the pure oil.

Thereafter, the oil-presser entrusted the oil to the torch-bearer of the king. The torch-bearer moistened a piece of cloth with that oil and he arranged the torches and set them alight. Slowly and gradually that oil turned into the shape of fire and as a result of it, many wonderful lights appeared. The other officers turned to seize wax. Where there were beehives, they seized them and extracted pure wax from them. The other party became busy with the purchase of the fats of animals, and after seizing the candles and the fats of high and superior quality entrusted them to the torch-bearers of the king.

That party of torch-bearers worked out wonderful plans. They prepared candles of different sizes and shapes and kindled them in the court of the king. In all these activities the real purpose was the illumination of the court of the king and nothing else. Nay, in fact, the only object was to please the heart of the king and to manifest his beauty. These changing and different conditions would not have been there if there had been no preparatory causes for them. Moreover, the "Hubbiyyah point"[1] was shifting from state to state till it reached the lights and wherever it reached them it heard the address: "Had it not been for you, I would not have created the heavens". And wherever it reached, the confiscating officers accompanied it, and the treatment of every artisan with honour became binding. Superiority and beauty accompanied it both in form and in indications.

Sat' 32

When the perfect man journeying through the non-material world enters into the Great Body he begins to travel through its various revolutions and states till he comes back to the place he has descended from. At his very beginning in that travel he is tightly connected with the "Hubbiyyah point". It is so because his settlement in a fixed place in the Holy Fold and the great works on account of which he had to remain in the (everlasting) world were all desired. And all this is included in the Universal Order and then in the Divine Providence. Thus, by his taking the first step in his travel through the revolutions and states, all the processes he had to pass through in the World of Divinity became represented. And there it became clear that in such-and-such a process he will be of this attribute and in such-and-such a process of another attribute. He becomes characterised by all the preparatory things in every process which will

---

[1] This refers to the well-known Divine Tradition: "I was a hidden treasure".

be the cause of his external existence there, and by the
capabilities which are required in that process, in order
that he may create a capability in himself for attaining
the perfection of the next process. All this became
represented in the world of Divinity.[1] This same
"Hubbiyyah point" made this requirement of the same
type as the one mentioned in the simile in the preceding
Sat'.

At present the grain of sesame is green and the skilled
cultivator knows well that there are certain causes useful
to this process which require that the sesame plant be
properly watered so that the oil in it may fully increase,
and that there are certain other causes which work contrary to that. Therefore, he works upon a plan, so that
the sesame be acquired as desired. In the same manner,
the Divine plan in the case of the perfect man gives rise to
such occasions, such transformations and such causes
which lead to the desired object. "I was a prophet while
Adam was still in water and clay"[2] is a reference to the
process of the offspring.

When the "Hubbiyyah point" entered into the human
process, the causes which led to the goodness of the child,
who happens to be a symbol of the good condition of his
parents, were taken into consideration. What mystics
write, namely, that the light of Muhammad had first
appeared in the forehead of Adam, then in the forehead
of Seth, and so on and on till it appeared in the forehead
of 'Abdul-Muttalib and then in the forehead of 'Abdullah
is true. And what has come in the Tradition that "I am
the son of noble, pure women", and in the Tradition

---

[1] The existence is of many stages. The plane and the process are
also from the stages of existence in different respects. Existence has
one particular stage which is called a plane. Whenever a thing progresses in the 'plane', it is called a 'process', just as happens in
transformation and change. In a process, capability is produced and
that goes to help towards the production of another capability. All
these processes and capabilities become represented in the world of
Divinity.

[2] This refers to the saying of the Holy Prophet.

elsewhere that "When people were divided into two groups, God made me in the better of them", and in some other Tradition that "God chose Arabs and from them chose the tribe of Mudar and from it He chose its descendant branch Kinanah and from Banu Kinanah He chose the tribe of Quraish", is all an exposition of this knowledge.

When this perfect one appeared in the human process, the "Hubbiyyah point" appeared in the most perfect form. Then various kinds of blessings and miracles began to appear from him. This meaning went on increasing till the desired object came to completion by the raising of the prophet. After the Holy Prophet, that same "Hubbiyyah point", through the hands of Caliphs, became the cause for the completion of the Divine promises. After that, this same "Hubbiyyah point" shifted to the Intermediary World, and there it facilitated the meeting of the holy soul of the Holy Prophet with the Exalted Companion and became its focus. And it became the cause of the appearance of the Great Intercession on the Day of Last Judgment. In truth, this treatment is shown to every perfect one, but the appearance of the "Hubbiyyah point" in every perfect one is, however, according to the shining of his Pure Intellect, and to the great and important works desired by his appearance in the world. God says: "Allah knows best where to place His message".[1]

Sat' 33

Journey and travel (*Sair wa suluk*) according to the veridical vision can have no cause other than this, that the Will (of God) appeared to the effect that such a person should reach such a place in the plane of the Holy Fold. When this Will was made, the Divine powers began to change that man from state to state and interfere in the causes suitable to it (Will), so that he might shift

---

[1] Qur'an, Surah Al-Anam, V. 125.

from this world according to that part of the plane of the Holy Fold. Some of these changes take place without his intention and desire.[1] They inspire some persons with the result that they intentionally perform acts of worship, undergo both bodily and spiritual exercises and become fit for that place. "And He takes (some) from you as witnesses"[2] carries this meaning. And this is the secret of the priority of "He loves them" to "They love Him".[3] In certain cases, if there happens to be a pure person of such rank that they would like to bring him to that plane of the Holy Fold, they inform him (of it) either through discernment (*Firasat*) or by a dream. "They have good news in the worldly life."[4] In certain other cases, they inspire him with thoughts of longing to travel this path, as "Every one is given a facility to what he is created for".[5]

Many persons who do not know the plane they are going to and the Divine Plan which has become the cause of such inspiration, vainly imagine that they have travelled through by their own efforts and by means of this travel have reached the desired goal.

Sat' 34

Some people are under the impression that the union with God which is the ultimate goal of the journey and travel of the mystics is not other than the correction of thought. The real object, in fact, is the attainment of gnosis (*M'arifat*) and nothing else. The path of gnosis means to divest thought from every thing else. If self-disciplining is desired, it can be acquired in this way, as the divestiture of thought can never be achieved without little eating, less association with people and little sleep.

[1] Some changes, according to the capability of that person, are brought about by the Divine powers without any effort on his part.
[2] Qur'an, Surah Al-'Imran, V. 139.
[3] Ibid. Al-Ma'idah, V. 54.
[4] Ibid. Yunus, V. 64.
[5] This is a reference to the Tradition.

In my opinion what is established and confirmed is this, that by the real object is meant the attainment of a certain part of the plane of the Holy Fold which the Divine powers have fixed for him. The path to this real object requires a change of the bestial qualities, so that the annihilation of the dark existence and survival by spiritual existence could be achieved. If the man is one of the select saints, another change besides this one is also desired in his case, so that the annihilation of the spiritual existence and the survival by the reality of Divinity (*Lahut*), which means the prevalence of the existence of the Real (God) upon your existence, is achieved.

When the human soul possesses both the faculties (intellectual as well as practical), the recitation of litanies, the contemplation and the divestiture of thought also become conditions of travel, as half of the desired object depends upon them. The parable of the journey and travel is like this one: "We kindled fire below ice till it melted and became water. After that, from water air was formed".

Sat⁴ 35

Sometimes a certain person among men appears to be perfect in respect of qualities worthy of consideration in the worldly life. For example, he is beautiful, eloquent, brave, strong, industrious, highly fortunate, dignified, powerful in executing his orders, possessing servants, wealth and children. But when he shifts from this world to the Intermediary, no excellence remains with him. He turns destitute and is in a bad condition. "Verily God does not look to your forms and wealth, but He looks only to your intentions and actions." Similarly sometimes there happens to be a person who shows signs of sainthood; such as that when he concentrates upon a certain work, it takes place in the external world according to the intention. He discloses things of the future and exercises his influence upon the hearts of travellers (*Salikin*) and so on. People consider him as excelling another saintly person from whom the manifestation of such signs is not equal to his. But when they both reach the part of the plane of the "Holy Fold" which was their share, the excelled one becomes the excelling one and the excelling one, the excelled. Sometimes, though a person has corrected his imaginative faculty while contemplating (*Muraqibat*) but has not corrected his practical faculty, he has not adequately suppressed his bestiality, and his animal faculty has not been sufficiently restrained as yet. When he reaches the plane of the "Holy Fold", half of his face appears beautiful and half ugly. "They have mixed a good action with an evil one." Therefore in journey and travel that man should be taken as a guide who may be aware of the "Holy Fold" and not a person from whom many revelations and miracles are seen.

Sat' 36

By manifestation (*Tajalli*) is meant a creation (*Makhluq*) which imitates some attributes of the Creator and on account of it, some things of God are attributed to it. To explain further, when a man sees God in a dream in the form of a king, sitting on a throne, with a crown on his head, then that form is without doubt a creation. The matter of its creation is the stored-up knowledge of the seer, and the place of its creation is his mind (*Khiyal*). Now, this form in respect of connections which are worthy of consideration in the science of the interpretation of dreams, indicates the meaning of kingdom and the execution of orders, and that is the attribute of God. Both in the Law and in the common language it can be said: "I have seen God in a dream" or that "God said so and so".

Thus this form is a creation which has become the revealer of God in relation to some of His attributes, and on that account sight, command and the prohibition of the Creator are attributed to it. But if it does not reveal some attributes of the Creator, then it cannot be called a manifestation. Just as if one were to see in his dream a stone or a tree which might not reveal some attributes of God (as happens in most of the dreams of the common people), then that cannot be a manifestation. If an angel and a soul of a saint were to reveal some attributes of God in the external world or in a dream, but their action is not found attributable to God, then it also cannot be a manifestation.

The manifestation in this sense has been proved to be true. Its proof has been established in the Law. God says: "When his Lord manifested His glory to the mountain",[1] namely, upon the mountain, as the first manifestation was made on the tree. The Holy Prophet has also said, "I saw my Lord in a most beautiful form". In a Tradition referring to the Judgment Day are many words which point to this fact.

Sat' 37

There are many Divine Manifestations in the world. Some take place in the mind of man in sleep or in wakefulness, just as happened in the case of the Holy Prophet when he saw his Lord in the most beautiful form; and some appear in the external world, just as happened in the case of the Prophet Moses. The truth about the manifestation in the external world is this, that there takes place a Divine Will regarding the education of a servant and for the administration of a certain affair in such-and-such a manner. Consequently, this Will falls from the Great Manifestation like a spark and then, having created latitude in the Sublime Assembly and thereafter having joined the similitudinary faculties with itself, comes down on a certain place in the earth. Here it conquers the earthly causes through expansion, contraction and transformation till a form suitable to what was imagined by the Sublime Assembly appears in this place. The element which accepts the form of this kind the most is the air, and in relation to accepting expan-

---

[1] Qur'an, Surah Al-A'raf, V. 143.

sion and contraction it is again the same air which among all other causes is the most potent cause. Some air is dense and some is thin and a powerful wind renders the dense air still more so and prepares it as a place for the reflection of the light of the rays of the sun or of the moon—or of something else. This collective form imitates some of the attributes of God by its own radiancy.

Sometimes, on account of certain causes, a light or a glitter appears in some of the bodies. The Divine grace in this case strikes and then effects expansion in some of the hidden causes and gives rise to a wonderful beauty and a rare splendour in that place. That beauty and splendour through the connections of the interpretation reveal some of the attributes of God as does a dream.

Sat' 38

The original source of every kind of manifestation which takes place in the world is the Great Manifestation. Its relation to this Great Manifestation is like the relation the fleshly form of Zaid, whose human soul (*Nafs-i-natiqa*) is the Great Manifestation, has to the forms of Zaid on paper made of different colours, particular lines and the specified figures which, in a way, signify the corporeal existence of Zaid, his clothes and his outward appearance. In the same manner, the Great Manifestation is a suitable form of God, while all other manifestations are giving information of the Great Manifestation, and are revealing some of its attributes and forms.[1]

An elucidation of this summary is this, that it is however not necessary that the relation between the two things should be in quality and quantity and in no other respect. When we think of an abstract (*Mujarrad*) in the perceptive faculty, a conceptual or imaginary form

[1] The Great Manifestation is, however, a concept, while Reality is beyond any concept, and is incomprehensible.

arises from it. The imprinted form of one abstract, however, differs from the imprinted form of another abstract. One is peculiar to one abstract and the other is peculiar to another abstract. This peculiarity is not there because of the resemblance of the colours or on account of any agreement in quantities. In like manner we think of the absolute unknown, absolute non-existence and an agreement between two contraries. From each one of them a form is drawn different from the form of the other. Thus, the peculiarity of one to the first and the peculiarity of another to the second is determined, but this peculiarity is not determined by material accompaniments. From this it can be found that the relation of the abstract to things drawn in the mind and imagination is not by way of any resemblance and similarity.

In short, the Abstract pure through Primal Providence, without the requirement of a particular process, produces some relation with the Great Manifestation in the sense that has been mentioned in the parable. And where the form of this manifestation spreads in the world, there the capability of the process, however, plays its part. In a round and straight mirror the actual form of Zaid is reflected; but in a concave, long and wide mirror his reflected form is different from his natural constitution, even though it is certainly his form. Similarly, the Great Manifestation bears an essential relation to the Abstract pure. Every form which spreads in the various parts of the universe imitates only one attribute of the Great Manifestation, and is surrounded by certain affections occasioned by the nature of the place and the unexpected situations. What a great difference between the two! Thus, one of the signs of the existence of the Great Manifestation is this, that it is the source for the particular manifestations in the universe.

Sat‘ 39

When a Muslim recites litanies such as "There is no god but Allah," "Allah is the great," "Glory be to Allah" and such other words as these, he certainly understands an Essence in them, and ascribes these attributes to the same Essence. Thus unavoidably a form of the subject matter becomes present in the mind. And this form in one of his inner faculties, such as the comprehensive and the thinking, is itself of God. When he remembers this meaning frequently, that weak form gains strength till at times it settles in his mind even without the use of the words of these litanies, then disappears and afterwards reappears. When he remembers too much, that form settles down in one of his inner faculties in such a way that while going along a road, in eating, drinking and in all other conditions, it does not pass away from his intellectual faculty, and no occupation stops its presence. It becomes like this: "A person places a bucket full of water on his head, and while going on the road talks to someone, and whatever he wants to do in his house also engages his attention. In this state he intends that he will use a portion of this water for cooking food, a portion for washing clothes and a portion he will keep ready for drinking". All these divided forms are, however, represented in the intellect of this man, and his comprehensive faculty has a scope for them all. Similarly this mystic retains his contemplation of his own Principle in general, throughout his conditions and activities. After this he makes further progress, and slowly and gradually repels these divided attentions, and with one faculty brings all the other divided faculties back.

My heart had many a divided desire
They all united when my eye fell on thee.

After that he makes progress even in this union. In the beginning he finds that he is exclusively devoted to the side of the Real object, and in the end he forgets himself. This state is called disappearance and nothingness. Its relation to the Abstract is like the relation of sight to the object of space, when our eye falls on a visible object, and the common sense extracts a form from it in spite of its being mingled with the material accompaniments of the space. Its relation to other things which are lying on its left and right, such as colours, figures, states and such similar things, is like the relation the sight has to the objects of space. We call this sight.

In a similar manner, the mystic is applied to the Abstract Real and the comprehensive faculty is dropped off, just as the common sense was dropped off in the parable mentioned above. In short, the form in the comprehensive faculty which reveals the Abstract is the shadow of the Great Manifestation in its (comprehensive faculty's) mirror.

Sat' 40

The mystics (Ahl-i-walayat) are transformed from quality to quality. It is like this: "They kindled fire below ice till it melted and became water. After that, the kindling continued till the coolness of water disappeared and it became tepid. After that, the kindling continued further till it became hot. Thereafter, the kindling continued still further till it acted like fire, in cooking, in giving pain and in raising a blister on the body of man". All these changes do not take water out of its reality, but they bring its reality near to the reality of fire. Similarly, the annihilation and the survival of mystics do not mean a going out of humanity, but rather removing far away some of the human attributes resembling those of animals and beasts, and instead bringing near some of the human attributes which resemble those of angels. After that the mystic rises to the rank of the Divine omnipotence. Now, we have come to the actual topic. This resemblance cannot be established without the one with which it is made. And that one is the Holy Fold. This movement which comes in the Category "Kaif" (Quality) certainly has a polarity, and that polarity is the attribute of the Holy Fold.

Sat' 41

When common Muslims and others say "God", a clue

towards the All-embracing, Administrative Reality takes place in their perceptive faculty, because the pronouncement upon an object without the occurrence of its thought to the mind is not correct. And these thoughts in the mind of a person are the effects of many causes. One of those causes is the Holy Fold and the Sublime Assembly.

God has created the Sublime Assembly for the purpose that it should influence the Great Person, that is to say humanity, as the intellectual faculties influence the small person, namely one of the individuals of the human species. Just as man's intellectual faculties rule his body, similarly the Sublime Assembly rules human species and its every individual. When a belief of fear or of shame settles down in the mind of a man, his colour goes pale, his appetite is lost, and his body begins to shiver. All this is the effect of the intellectual faculties on the body of man. In like manner the inspirations of the Sublime Assembly have an effect on human individuals.

In short, this intellectial form "God" which we call a thought occurring to the mind, when it is deeply thought over, appears to be a shadow of the Divine form which is established in the Sublime Assembly as it is established in the minds of perfect human beings. Some individuals (after their death) join the Sublime Assembly and are counted in it. From them also a ray of light falls upon the minds of men like the reflection of sunshine on the clouds of different qualities in the air. This ray becomes the cause of the thoughts of this All-embracing, Administrative Reality occurring to the mind. If this ray were not to spread in the air, no person on earth would utter the word "God", and recognise Him through it. All this is one of the blessings of the Divine Secret (Manifestation), shown by means of its influencing the spirits of the Sublime Assembly.

Sat' 42

When God in His Primal Providence made the species.

of man to appear, and made it as the best of species, he called man His vicegerent, in the sense that he combines two parts, the angelic and the human. In respect of his human part, it became necessary that this also should be caused to appear, so that when he was to put on the material dress he should have a source, and that source is the elements. He should have also a comfortable place, and that comfortable place is eating and drinking. In addition to these, he should have a wide field for free movement, and that is speaking, seeking authority, making houses and such other necessary works of life. Similarly, in respect of his angelic part, it became necessary that a source be made to appear for him. And that source is the human soul, which has penetrated the well balanced "Nasmah". It rules it by pouring into it the intellectual and practical faculties. Besides, he should have a comfortable place, and that comfortable place is the Divine treasure named the Sublime Assembly, so that the human soul should bear resemblance to it (treasure). Thus he succeeds in acquiring certain secret sciences either through sight or dream or by means of an inspiration, and this becomes a balance for the correction of his practical faculties. Whenever any ugly act is done by him, and his soul on that account falls down from the (human) specific equilibrium, there appears a dislike in that treasure. And whenever he performs a good action, his resemblance to the Sublime Assembly increases correspondingly, and an appreciation flows from it, like the effect left by food and drink, nutrition, on the health of the bodies of men. Apart from that, he should also have a wide field for free movement, and that wide field is the "stations" (*Muqamat*) of the mystics and the religious ranks, such as those of a chief (*Qutub*), of a spiritual guide and of a reformer. Just as when a foot falls on burning charcoal or ice, we feel pain from heat or cold in our brain, similarly whenever any human being does an act of disobedience or performs an act of obedience, there appears an appreciation or depreciation apposite to that act in the Sublime Assembly. And the plan of the

Universal nature requires that that hatred or love should flow like water towards the spirits (*Nufus*) of the Lower Assembly and the intellects of the creatures possessing will, and that the worldly reward may be established. In the hereafter, these very inspirations will flow towards those angels who possess the similitudinary powers very strongly, and there that becomes the cause of punishment and reward.

Sat' 43

Some members of the Sublime Assembly are spirits connected with the fixed stars. Some of them are spirits puffed into luminous bodies near the time of the strongly auspicious conjunctions of the stars, like the conjunction of the planets. By luminous bodies are meant the fine elements in which the essence (*Juhar*) of air dominates, and which are not seen by the faculty of seeing. Some pure spirits of men also join the Sublime Assembly. The place of the Sublime Assembly is neither in the up nor in the down, but is joined to the Holy Fold. Wherever they be, they are in each others' company.

The Lower Assembly is the particular spirits puffed into airy bodies near the time of the particular, auspicious conjunctions of the stars, such as when Venus and Jupiter stand in a favourable position over against each other, as these are blessed in their essential attributes and the unexpected forms. This body is of various classes. Every class is an army of that star, the power of the auspiciousness of which happens to be dominating at the time of puffing the soul. These armies, however, call for a detailed account, and this treatise has no scope for that. "No one knows the armies of your Lord but He Himself."[1] This body is like an intermediary between the minerals and the animals, and has no fixed constitution as is required by a specific form. One is like a globe,

---

[1] Qur'an, Surah Al-Mudaththir, V. 31.

another like a turnip, a triangle and a rectangle and so on.

During the conjunctions which resemble the conjunctions requiring the puffing of their souls, there comes an increase in their bodies, not through the nutritive or retentive power. Their movements, according to the requirement of the inspiration that flows from the Divine Assembly, are like the natural flow of water; and the requirement of the nature of airy bodies and that of the celestial powers also prevails. Thus, they move when wind moves, just as man moves by his feet. For an action which is agreeable to their nature, thousands collect, and in consequence, peace of mind, angelic inspirations and premonitions suitable to their nature flow from them. By "Contention" of the Sublime Assembly is meant that every class of them has been created with a certain faculty, and it determines the reward of men according to that faculty. And their course according to the requirement of their faculties is, however, different. This same difference is termed "Contention", till the Administrator of the heavens and the earth after effecting agreement between all the faculties, sends an order in a manner in which he, after effecting an agreement between the form of the seer and the picture of the mirror, shows a specified form.

Sat' 44

Consider the universe as an embroidered carpet, in which the skilled artisan has not drawn a circle on one side without drawing a similar one on the other side as well, and for every flower he has fixed a size. In like manner, the Administrator of the heavens and the earth (God) has not left Venus to face Mars in the horoscope of the mind (*Nafs*) of one man, but He has left Mars also to face Venus in the horoscope of the mind of another man, so that the affair of love between the two may be arranged. Similarly, He has not placed the subjugation of the sun in one mind but He has placed in equal proportion the power of being subjugated in the other mind. "That is the decree (of Him), the Exalted in might, the All-knowing."[1]

When the time of the appearance of the predications (*Ahkam*) of this horoscope comes, an inspiration flows to the side of the lower angels and the animals possessing the power of will to the effect that they should cause that intended order (*Nazm*) to appear. Similarly, when the peremptories (*Quat'a*) come, they should prepare the causes of death or of destruction, and so on.[2] These inspirations are current in all the conditions, whether they be good or bad. All these are the particular causes serving the creative order (of God).

When the Grace flows from the singular point towards the Holy Fold and the Sublime Assembly, the Divine powers pour it down into the pure mind (Prophet) for the sake of improving the order of the world, for bringing human individuals near to the human specific equilibrium and for delivering them from injustice, from the chastisement of the grave and from the punishment of the Day of Last Judgment; and they give him support for the completion of that light (of guidance). That becomes a universal cause and the Legislative intention. These angels who are the servants of the command of Legislation are superior and most perfect, and in point of light are nearer to God than the angels to whom the affairs of creation are assigned. However, at the time of bringing victory to the prophet, both the armies join together and in consequence wonderful blessings appear.

Sat' 45

The Abstract has a peculiar relation to this fixed part in Shakhs Akbar but not like the relation the substance has to the accident or the accident had to the substance,

---

[1] Qur'an, Surah, Yasin, V. 38.

[2] *Qat'a* (Pl. *Quat'a*) means something certain, and here it refers to the cause of death.

so that a word in the language was invented for it. People sought for that a near simile and the clearest metaphor. Every person brought a word. One said a "Person of the Sacred Trinity", and an "Idol", another gave the name of "Incarnation" and the third said "The representation of the Deity in the form of man" (Anthropomorphism). All these words do bring the desired object near in one way and remove it in another way; but the corruption caused by them is much greater than the reformation worked by them. It is so because the common people, having invented many forms of infidelity and gross ignorance, have fallen into a deep chasm from which they can never rise.

When the Administrator of the heavens and the earth (God) manifested His grace in the garment of words and letters in the Divine Books, that grace made a natural flow. All the past evils became represented before His eye, and then some other way was fixed for the guidance of people. That is the interpretation of the Throne, the Owner of the Throne and of the Sitting upon the Throne. This sitting upon, however, took place after the creation of the seven heavens. The reason being, that this middle point which is one in Shakhs Akbar became fixed in it after its entire completion, just as the centre becomes fixed after the completion of a spherical object. God says: "He created seven heavens and then sat upon the Throne".[1]

One body of the angels which is foremost in the Holy Fold is named the "Bearers of the Throne", another one is termed "Hovering around the Throne", and another one is called the "High-ranking".

It has been said in some of the commentaries of the Traditionists that the Bearers of the Throne are four angels. One is in the shape of a man and that is the intercessor of men, another is in the form of a bull and that is the intercessor of the animals, the third is in the form of a vulture and that is the intercessor of the birds and the

---

[1] Qur'an, Surah Al-Furqan, V. 59.

fourth is in the shape of a lion and that is the intercessor
of the beasts of prey. It has been related in the Musnad of
Darimi that when once the following verse of the poet
Umayyah bin Abi'l-salt was recited before the Holy
Prophet, he said that he had spoken the truth.

A man and a bull are by its right foot
The vulture and the watchful lion are by its left.

On certain occasions the Holy Prophet had seen them
in the form of mountain goats. All these are wonders of
the Similitudinary World, and their comparison is, however, given according to the essential relation and the
unexpected accidental resemblance. God knows best.

In reality, this middle part in Shakhs Akbar has no
aspect of aboveness or of belowness. It is spiritual.
However, when it is more peculiar to the spirit of the
crystalline sphere which is the greatest heavenly body,
the people in the Divine Laws attribute aboveness to
God. It is just like the human soul which bears greater
resemblance to the airy spirit. The source of the airy
spirit is the clot of blood. People on that account
attributed the human soul to this clot of blood. The
Holy Prophet has said, "There is a clot of blood in the
body. If it is sound the body is sound, and when it
becomes unsound the body becomes unsound. Remember, it is the heart". God says, "The eyes are not blind
but the hearts which are in the breasts are blind".[1]

Now, when the "Sitting upon the Throne" took place
after the creation of the seven heavens, nay, even after
"He has inspired every heaven with its affairs",[2] after
the extension of the earth (by Him), after the creation of
the profitable things in the earth, and after the formation
of the three kingdoms of nature (animal, vegetable and
mineral) in it, there came the question of Abu Razin
'Uqaili: "Where was our Lord before He created His
creation?" He (the Holy Prophet) replied, "He (God)

---

[1] Qur'an, Surah Al-Hajj, V. 46.
[2] Ibid. Ha'Mim, V. 12.

was in a black cloud, where there was no air above or
below it". It means, that His connection was kept with
the Rahmani soul, and it is this same connection which
has now appeared in the form of the "Sitting upon the
Throne".[1]

Sat' 46

God says: "God is the light of the heavens and the
earth, the parable of His light is as if there were a niche
and within it a lamp, the lamp enclosed in glass, the glass
is as if it were a brilliant star, lit from a blessed tree, an
olive, neither of the east nor of the west, whose oil is
about to burst into luminosity though it is scarcely
touched by fire, light upon light. God doth guide whom
He will to His light".[2]

If the misunderstanding of those who deeply think over
this verse does not stand in the way, its meaning is most
clear in explaining the Divine Secret. That same
Abstract Reality is the light of the heavens and the
earth, but by means of the Divine Secret in the manner
the parable has been given. This is like our human soul
which sees by means of a faculty which is hidden in the
crystalline lens, the eye; it hears by means of a faculty
which is spread in the auditory nerve of the ear; it
catches things by means of a faculty which is spread in
the hands; and it moves on by means of a faculty which
is placed in the feet.

The description of the light of God in the heavens and
the earth is like the description of a niche . . . right up to
the end of the verse. Here transposition has taken place,
and that is what the language of the unmixed, pure
Arabic requires, just as you have understood in the commentary of the verse "If one of the two were to make a
mistake, the one may remind the other".[3] The cause of

[1] For Nafs Rahmani, see Sat' No. 2.
[2] Qur'an, Surah Al-Nur, V. 35.
[3] Ibid. Al-Baqarah, V. 282.

transposition is this, that the course of discourse here is meant to explain the penetration of the light of God in the heavens and the earth like the spread of the light of a lamp in a niche. The rest of the discourse is the completion of the subject set for discussion.

The real object is this, that the quality of the light of God is like the quality of the lamp which is placed in the chandelier and which again is placed in the niche. That lamp is being kindled with the olive oil taken from the olive tree which is neither in the east nor in the west, but is in the middle of the trees. The sunshine keeps it (tree) pleasant both in the morning and the evening. The oil of that tree would well-nigh shine out even though the fire had not yet touched it. This lamp is a light upon light.

By lamp is meant the wick which on account of the oil is kindled in the chandelier. Just as the fire of the lamp continues in the wick by the oil and the oil is its vehicle, similarly the Divine Form continues by the part of the Similitudinary World which exists in the middle, and which is like the pleasant olive tree, neither of the east nor of the west. This means that it is neither so much an Abstract as to accept the grace of the Origin in the beginning nor so much a materiality as to throw off its grace in the end, but is in the middle of them. That part bears complete resemblance to the Abstract pure, and on that account has become Its vehicle and mirror. In the various parts of Shakhs Akbar no part has the capability of becoming the mirror but this one. Thus it is just the Abstract pure and Pure light. When the Divine Manifestation became set over it, it turned light upon light. Just as that shining wick is in the glass which is extremely bright, similarly is that Divine Manifestation in the Holy Fold. The whole of it (Holy Fold) turned into its colour in one way or the other, as if it became that very Divine Manifestation itself. That glass is in the niche, namely the arch, which is the place for placing the chandelier. Just as the spreading rays in the chandelier have taken over the whole of the arch, reached all its sides and have turned them all bright by their own light, similarly the rays have radiated from the Holy Fold towards all the things of the universe by means of the angels of both the Sublime and Lower Assemblies. And after having ruled them all, having brought them under the force of their command and having dispelled the darkness of all, made then resemble the Real Good. On that account, the resemblance of Shakhs Akbar to the *summum bonum* became complete.

For further information on this
subject please write to:—

THE SOCIETY FOR SUFI STUDIES
P.O. BOX 43   LOS ALTOS
CALIFORNIA 94022   USA

Waliullah, Shah

Sufism and the Islamic
Tradition